When Every Day Was Summer

Boyhood and youth in a rural community 1920-1939

4000006?

J. E. Bowman

OWL
BOOKS

First published November 1989 by
Owl Books,
P.O. Box 60, Wigan WN1 2QB

British Library Cataloguing in Publication Data

Bowman, J.E. (1920-)
When Every Day Was Summer.
1. Lancashire. Fylde (District) Social life 1900-.
Biographies
I. Title
942.7'662082'0924

ISBN 0-9514333-2-6

Design and typesetting by Graphic Design, Wigan.

Printed and bound in Great Britain.

To my children Susan, Geoffrey and John;
and to my grand-children Emma, Sally,
Alan and Richard and hopefully to
successive generations.

"For though we slepe, or wake, or rome, or ryde,
Ay fleeth the tyme, it wil no man abyde.
And though your grene youthe floure to day,
In crepith age alway as stille as stone,
And deth menaceth every age, to slay
Ech man and al, for ther escapith none.
And as certeyn, as we knowe every one
That we shal deye, so uncerteyn we alle
Be of that day that deth shal on us falle".

The Clerkes Tale
Geoffrey Chaucer

ACKNOWLEDGEMENTS

IT has been my good fortune to have been able to draw upon the amazingly retentive memory of Mr. J.B. Bowman, a resident of Hambleton. Mr. Bowman, now an octogenarian, is my Uncle Ben, who pops up from time to time in my story. Being an expert rustic raconteur, a species fast becoming extinct, the material which he has provided first-hand has proved so valuable that this book is as much his as it is mine.

Mrs. J. Parkinson, Shirley, who is his daughter, has also read my manuscript and has been most helpful in assembling controversial details.

To Mrs. Beatrice Singleton I am also indebted for supplying and verifying various items.

Ben Wilmot, an old school-mate of Baines Grammar School, has been most forthcoming in jogging my memory, providing material and reminiscences and giving generous encouragement and welcome constructive criticism.

Mrs. Agnes Greenbank deserves a special commendation for having once again grappled with drafts written in my atrocious long-hand. She has emerged, battered but triumphant, clutching the completed typescript.

My wife Joan, supportive as ever, has once again accepted my endeavour with placid forbearance; and if at times she has been worn down by frequent repetitions of variations on the same themes, she has been kind enough and skilful enough not to show it.

CONTENTS

Prologue

The Characters Emerge   1

A Disturbing Revelation   14

Supernatural Diversion   27

A Confession of Practical Inadequacy   39

Customs and Classroom   46

Artistry and Ailments   56

From Harvest to the Academic   64

Prelude to Christmas   76

Farewell to Innocence   82

Of Sport, Bomb Making, Tommy and Little Joe   88

Black Puddings and Miss Elsie West   99

The Cow   108

The Passing of my Benefactor   113

The River   119

Land Hill Farm   129

Ned Was a Good Milker   139

A Brief Dissertation on Schooling   147

Sorrow and Joy   157

The Demon Intrudes   163

'Let Joy be Unconfined'   170

The Formidable Critchleys   176

Alongside The Men   184

The Passing Bell Tolls   192

A Visionary Tour   208

The Demon Wins   215

Family Tree

CONTENTS

Preface

Prologue

MY mother had become one of yesterday's children. She was in the act of joining her parents and relatives, former playmates, all the acquaintances which she had loved or formed an affection for during her long life.

Those lying so still here in their last resting places were of all ages, from the very young to the very old. Death does not discriminate. One by one, those round about had been nudged off the conveyor-belt we call life and were now members of that tightly-knit community sleeping eternally within the boundaries of Hambleton churchyard.

My mother had always known that it was to this place that she would make her last journey. It was in the order of things. Generation succeeding generation, members of her family had been borne shoulder-high to their graves. There was never any doubt that she would wish to break, or would break the continuity.

In the old days, as a last gesture of dignity and respect, coffins were carried shoulder-high, sometimes for considerable distances, with relays of bearers in attendance to take over at intervals. My grandfather's remains had been taken in such a way, right from Crooklands Cottage, down Market Street, up Church Lane and up the path into the Church.

Myself and my elder son leading as bearers, we had carried my mother's coffin on our shoulders out of the Church and had wended our slow, mournful way up the path to the open grave. My wife, the rest of my family and my mother's other relations were at the forefront of the numerous mourners who had come to pay their last respects.

For my mother, her last years had been a heavy burden. It had not been easy either for those closest to her who were forced to stand by helpless and witness her slow deterioration.

After living with me and my family in Leeds where she had never really settled, she had returned to Hambleton to a bungalow on a complex reserved for elderly people. There she was content enough had it not been for the double misfortune which beset her. Her eye-sight and hearing worsened until she was totally blind and very deaf. Remaining houseproud, she continued with her dusting and polishing until one day she fell off a small step-ladder. At this point it would have been better for her had she ceased to live, for from then onwards she was no longer self-reliant. The qualities of independence, determination, sheer strength of will now began to lose their power. At her own request she was admitted to the Princess Alexandra's Home for the Blind at South Shore, Blackpool. Whilst it must be stated categorically that only the highest praise is worthy of Matron and Staff of that establishment, it was not for one whose spirit had soared ever beyond restraint, who was totally unsuited and unprepared for communal living, who just had not the temperament nor the wish to adjust.

In the final period she lay, blind, deaf and incontinent, wishing that each hour would be her last. I think that this wish was echoed by the family. It certainly was by me.

What were to be my feelings when she had gone. Guilt-ridden of course, for not having enabled her to die at home, although there were several obstacles which had made this impracticable. Ultimately, however, every decision had been mine. I knew that as I stood as chief mourner in the Church or at the grave-side, there would be those few who were silent critics of my actions, for I had failed to subscribe to the Village custom of keeping relatives at home to the end. There was no definitive answer; for the merit in one course of action balanced the short-comings in the other and vice versa.

Standing by the grave-side on that chilly day of March, 1979, the countryside, save for one or two innovations which were aesthetically abhorrent, looked much the same as it had done when I was a child some fifty years ago, as it had done when my mother was a child, had done when her parents were young. Only the faces and costumes had changed, as the crops changed in their yearly processes of growing and ripening, within the predictable inevitability of the yearly cycle.

My short, intermittent visits over the last twenty years and my pre-occupation in other directions had not, up till now, permitted a closer observation. It was to come as a revelation and a disturbing one at that (though it was no revelation to those of my generation who had remained) that this village in which I had been born and reared was no more. It had gone. Another, very different appearance and character had been superimposed on its framework.

From the school-yard nearby, where my mother, clad in long frock and pinafore, had skipped so blithely in the days of her innocence and had joined in childish games, where I myself had cavorted in imitation of a horse and gyrated slowly in round dances of origin immemorial, where our own children had run about, agile and carefree, there arose the shrill sounds of today's children at play. Their young voices carried in the crisp air, over and away beyond the school-house garden which separated playground from churchyard. They integrated with our melancholy ritual. Thus youth and age, birth and death were juxtaposed in this poignant fashion.

We laid my mother with her parents and her Uncle Tom. It was as if they had been waiting expectantly for this reunion for the last forty years. This passing of time was of no consequence. The years were as nought. It seemed but a short while since I had stood at this grave-side, then newly opened, when I was a boy of twelve, yet it was forty seven years ago since we had buried my grandfather.

What did I really know about my grandparents, their successes and trials, their joys and disappointments? There was very little apart from the bits and pieces I had picked up whilst listening to their reminiscences on a winter's evening round the fire. What would my children and grand-children know of their parents and grandparents when we had gone. For their progeny we would be merely names in a hundred years time.

It was for them that I decided to write, in order that they can compare that which they themselves will be experiencing in their own environment, in their own age; an age which we can neither envisage nor comprehend.

LOCATION MAP

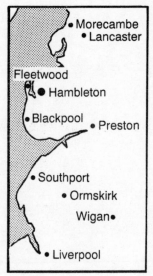

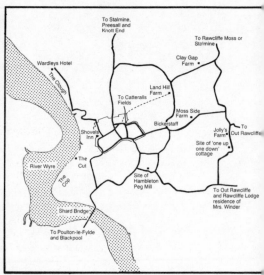

HAMBLETON

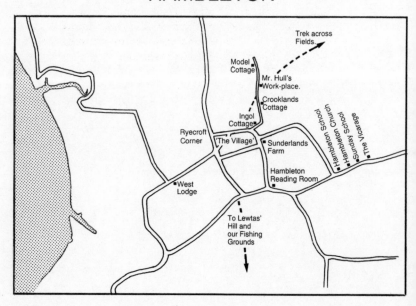

The Characters Emerge

AS I lay on the rug reading in front of a glowing coal fire my grandmother would flit about, sometimes stepping over me on one of her visits to the oven. The paraffin lamp was lit and the curtains drawn in the one living-room of our cottage. Here I was secure, snug and warm, with all the cares and despairs which make up adult life carefully hidden from me. The flickering flames of the fire and the relatively feeble rays from the lamp caused irregular shadows in far corners. These enhanced my comfort so much that I stretched and made feline movements of satisfaction.

It was early winter-time in the year 1930 and I was ten years of age.

The book I was reading was rather ambitious for one so young. It was George Eliot's 'Mill on the Floss'. Surely much of its deeper emotional content must have escaped me, or was I such a precocious child? At least I could read, had been reading fluently since I was six. I was fortunate in having an extensive library on which to draw. My mother worked as a domestic help at the vicarage two or three days a week. We were a loyal church-going family and the incumbent of the parish, the Rev. J. Gornall, M.A., had agreed that I could borrow his books. By my early teens I had read a good many of the accepted literary classics when I might well have been restricted to 'The Dandy'.

There were no distractions. Our very slender finances did not stretch to a wireless. Indeed, only the successful and wealthy householders possessed these revolutionary

1

inventions. The only one which I remember seeing was all exposed wires and black Bakelite dials and was unreliable in performance. I was privileged to apply the ear-phones and heard the faint strains of unidentifiable music apparently recorded through the hub-bub of an Australian sheep-fair. Inwardly, I was unimpressed. Television would have been met with spell-bound wonder, shunned by some as the creation of sorcerers, for the powers of evil were still hovering round and about in our country air. As for the dubious enchantments of computer games, I doubt whether our early twentieth century brains, attuned to operate at a more temperate pace, would have been sharp enough to cope. Had these essentials been available we would have been unable to operate most of them, for electricity supplied through the mains did not reach our Village until a few years later.

So I read voraciously, and for a change played with my cigarette cards, drew or painted, or constructed strange-shaped vehicles with my Meccano set.

My grandmother's frequent inspections of the contents of the oven, which was an integral part of the kitchen-range to the left of the raised fire-bars, were necessary to our general well-being and the most important operation in her domestic routine.

My grandmother, still at this time active enough, had been in service with "the gentry", among them the "Misses Barlow" who resided at 'Meadowcroft'. She had gathered further lady-like qualities and added them to what I later assessed was her natural gentility. Being an excellent cook she could coax succulence from the most common-place ingredients. Poor soul, it was also partially the case of necessity being the mother of invention, for she had managed for years on slender means. It was never that there was not enough to live on, for at feasts such as Christmas and when we had "company" our table groaned with the best of them. In normal times, however, we lived modestly, with nothing to throw away. "Waste not, want not", was my grandmother's watchword. Had we had a dustbin nothing edible would have been put in it.

Assisted sometimes by my mother, on the rare times when she was at home, for she always seemed to be out working, my grandmother would make bread and pies and more rarely, stew or meat and potato pie in a large brown glazed pot. We had a great earthenware kneading bowl which was filled with dough. When it was propped up on the fender in front of the fire for the dough to rise, I had to relinquish my favourite place on the rug and seek temporarily a less comfortable spot.

My fascinated wonder for the rapport between my grandmother and her oven remains to this day. She had no modern gauges to record temperatures. Yet with unerring judgement she would take her cloth and open the door. At that precise moment the cake or pie would be just ready for removal. Nothing was ever burnt, nothing underdone. Had there ever been such a catastrophe as a sagging bun or a slumped cake my grandmother would have gone into a decline.

Our rented cottage, a humble dwelling, sheltered five people. There was my grandfather, grandmother and great-uncle, my mother and myself. The three older ones were in their sixties and my mother was thirty-five. From time to time a sixth member of the family had to be squeezed in. He was my Uncle Ben, twelve years younger than my mother who was his sister.

I anticipated Uncle Ben's infrequent visits with great excitement as major events in my mundane calender. Uncle Ben worked on a farm in Out Rawcliffe, which is a sprawling neighbouring parish with no village as such. He "lived in" as unmarried farm servants did, laboured hard and long for very little, drank humility to the dregs and managed a few days off each year at Candlemas, the traditional time for signing on for the next year.

My grandfather John was a kindly sensitive man, ever mindful of those worse off than himself. The Bowman lineage had been in Hambleton for a long time. My grand-

My Uncle Ben,
rejoicing in his
young manhood,
about 1928.

father enjoyed the respect not only of his peers but also that of the Rev. Gornall. For had not my grandfather, who had a very fine tenor voice, sung in the church choir for nearly fifty years.

Whatever ambition my grandfather had possessed had been knocked out of him. Adversity had hunted him, tracked him down, and to adversity he had finally succumbed. It seemed that he had always been close to the land, working for his father and then in conjunction with his brothers Jonathan, Richard and Ben. Whatever had happened to the family association remained too convoluted for me to follow, but by the beginning of the First World War, only half a dozen years before I made my catastrophic and well-nigh unheralded entry, my grandfather was himself working as a farm-labourer for a Mr. Thomas Pye at Sunderlands Farm, just down the road from where we now lived.

The elder brother Jonathan had built himself a business and bought Land Hill Farm, whilst the other brothers had fallen out of the race. Doubtless farmers had made rich pickings, but for my harassed grandfather and his family the war years had been lean. Spanish influenza — a particularly virulent strain which carried off great numbers —

The three brothers and choir-members, taken outside Hambleton Church circa 1920. From left to right: Richard, John, Ben.

had almost put paid to my poor grandfather, already suffering from malnutrition aggravated by war-time rationing. He had never quite managed to achieve his former vigour.

So here was my tall, thin grandfather, with the drawn weathered face and the sad, sad eyes which had looked out on the world for a lifetime and assessed the greed, subterfuge and shabby lack of consideration without becoming embittered, now employed as a council worker. The job was a "cut above" the ordinary and the wage, about £2 a week, was quite good.

Often I have thought that had I been in his shoes, would I have managed to survive, to go on living, to want to live? I suppose that such stoicism was possible because there was at the end of the gruelling journey the promise of a place of perpetual restfulness called Heaven.

> *"Shall we gather at the River,*
> *The beautiful, the beautiful, the River,*

WHEN EVERY DAY WAS SUMMER

Shall we gather at the River,
That flows by the Throne of God",

sang my grandmother in her sweet, clear voice, when she
was feeling particularly uplifted. For their sakes I do hope
there is such a place and that they have found the relaxa-
tion they so richly deserve.

To sit on clouds, clad only in white night attire so closely
resembling shrouds, singing hymns from a limited repertoire, to the accompaniment of harps, never my favourite
instrument, repelled me rather than attracted. Much more
was I drawn to a warm place on the rug in front of the fire
than to unfurnished halls supported by cold marble col-
umns. There might be many mansions in my Father's house
but I did not want any part of them.

The Rev. Gornall preached with fervour that the love of
money was the root of all evil. I grant that it was his belief,
for though an educated man with qualifications which
could have led him far beyond his parish where he could
have had a much more lavish lifestyle, he displayed no
ambition greater than the shepherding of his modest rural
flock. He was safe, of course, in preaching his doctrine to
people like my grandfather, for they had few possessions
and no means of acquiring more.

Should I have been happier with far less? I think not, for
I have enjoyed the acquisition of worldly goods and unashamedly find comfort in having them round me. If my
grandfather fell sick his wage would stop. Failure to pay the
rent would result in eviction. What dreadful ogres leered
over his shoulders, ogres never to be seen by me, unless
some unforeseen economic disaster comes to all.

From Monday morning to Saturday noon, week in and
week out, my grandfather laboured in the country lanes.
His thin, sinewy arms and his gnarled old hands wielded
spade and shovel, sickle and scythe. He cleaned out ditches
and gullies, cut back the grass and ran out his line and
edged the roadside borders. Conscientious to a fault, his
work was perfection and everyone knew where John had
been. No stranger to bad weather, he was never known to

6

My Grandfather working very near to home — Crooklands Cottage in background — extreme right.

come home however severe the conditions. Rain, hail or sleet would find him crouched under sacking and his old top-coat, in the lea of some out-building, trying to light his pipe and snatch a draw; too fearful of authority to leave his appointed post. He was a solitary figure, always working alone unless some larger project like tar-spraying summoned him to join a group, when he would be ill-at-ease. Rarely was he known to lean on his shovel, and never for long.

Favoured was my grandfather in one respect. He knew not the hideous din of the mill, the dark depths of the mine. His was the freedom of the countryside, as yet unpolluted, as yet silent, save for animal sounds. He understood the changes of season, could predict weather from wind and moon and tides. Bird-song surrounded him in spring and summer and he had all the time in the world to think. Yet, before dawn on a Monday morning in winter, with the long, long week ahead and the sleet beating against the window-pane, did he consider himself the most fortunate of men? No-one ever knew, for he was never known to complain.

He would draw on his working trousers over the long woollen under-garments in which he slept, make his way quietly down the cold stairs to kindle a fire before a kettle could be boiled for his frugal breakfast and for the can of tea he took with him. An electric kettle and a toaster would have lightened his burdens enormously, but these modern aids were long into the future.

He walked everywhere. It was said that he had tried to master the bicycle and failed. His work sometimes took him to places which were miles away. As he was as punctilious at being at these places at the appointed times as he was of leaving them, and as his travelling time was in addition to the hours of his working day, he must have rejoiced at being assigned to tasks near to home quite as much as my grand-mother did.

In another place, under other conditions he might have been a gentle academician, offering a fund of wisdom and shrewdness, or he might have found joy in a career in music. As it was, fate had dealt him some bad hands.

He had lost the resilience to play back and recoup his losses. There was, however, never any doubt that he was in charge of the family. His rebukes, few in number, were more telling because they were gently given. I came to realise the latent power still in him which would rise to the surface if driven to the limit. In his younger days when roused he had been a formidable adversary. He never raised his hand to me, never caused me to have anything but the most profound respect for him. It turned out that he was my greatest benefactor and I worshipped him. I pressed my pale face to the window and looked at dusk for his homecoming. There never could have been a better friend than my grandfather.

The Characters Emerge

My Great-uncle Tom, if he had not already settled himself permanently in our cottage by 1930, was now about to do so. He was a bachelor who had worked with horses all his life. My first memory of him must have been two or three years earlier when he had come to visit his sister Elizabeth, my grandmother. He brought his lorry up our narrow lane and turned his team round. As the lorry was not laden, he had one of his huge shire horses in the shafts, with his trace-horse hooked behind. With a full load, his trace-horse would be hooked in front for greater drawing power. He would change their positions from time to time. He stood me by a huge foot, shaggy with white hair and bade me stroke it, assuring me that there was no danger of being crushed.

Mechanisation overtook him. When he came to us it was because progress had edged him out of a job. It was some years later before I learnt that he had suffered the heartbreak of parting with his beloved shires, having seen them off at the station, bound for a destination unknown.

Previously he and his shires had taken lorry-loads of potatoes to Fleetwood Market. In bad weather he would sit crouched at the front of his lorry under topcoats and sacks. He was a great believer in these hessian sacks for cover. Generally, they were popular forms of protection for farm-workers. With a full load, he would get off and walk to give a slight additional relief to his horses. I have heard it said that my great-uncle carried sweets to give to under-privileged children he passed on the way; and that he was not above sharing his dinner with needy youngsters. Nowadays, if a man were to make such gestures of kindness they would be interpreted differently. It may be that we have not come such a long way after all.

He was a very different character from my grandfather. In fact they were opposites except in one quality. They were both big-hearted, even if one of them did his best to hide it with irascibility. To look at my great-uncle when his barrier was up, which it often was, no-one would have suspected that he had a drop of gentleness in him.

His appearance on a weekday was an embarrassment to us. The casual clothes of old men of the period were not renowned for neatness of cut or even cleanliness. My great-uncle's outfit outdid them all. I suspect that there was somewhere in my great-uncle's lineage, built into his genes a tendency towards slovenliness, a lack of discipline in personal and domestic care which manifested itself as he grew old. My grandmother was very much the opposite and so was her daughter. In him it seemed as if several lifetimes of stored wilfulness had been collected and condensed. Or was it partly that he resented anything which represented or suggested affectation and struck against it?

His battered old trousers could never have belonged to him, for another person of his size could have been stuffed down the waistband. Though short of stature himself these trousers were even shorter and tapered with a fascinating rapidity until they ended abruptly by clutching his lower calves. Another quarter of a century was to pass before Max Wall adopted the same fashion. These lower garments were held up by braces. He called them 'gallases'. In place of a button a nail thrust in horizontally would serve just as well.

His clogs were all the more prominent and at least one of them would be laced with string. For some reason my great-uncle favoured bottling string. normally used to tie up bales of straw. It frayed easily so that he left a wake of strands and threads, unacceptable to the women of our household.

The sleeves of his union shirt were always rolled up. His arms and face were weathered to the colour of bog oak. For though a stranger to baths, the very mention of which he abhorred, he would take himself from time to time to the river and slake his arms and face in salt water. He firmly believed that any further ablutionary venture would remove the natural oils which protected his skin and kept him in good shape.

The hat put the finishing touches to his outdoor dress. As every hat must start off new, I can only assume that each rustic prepared his own head-gear in secret through a process of concentrated ill-treatment and exposure until it was fit to be worn in public. I never saw a labourer in those days in anything but the most decrepit of hats. For sheer outrageous decadence, my great-uncle outdid them all. Whereas my grandfather would be neatly shaved my great-uncle took a pride in always managing to have a three-day stubble on show.

Only on a Sunday morning was my great-uncle clean shaven except for his moustache, when he and my grandfather donned their stiff shirt fronts and ties, their dark suits, complete with waistcoats and, with shiny black boots gleaming, took themselves off to church, where my grandfather would settle in his privileged seat in the choir.

My Great-uncle Tom, taken about 1930.

Once my mother bought my great-uncle a neck-tie for his birthday. It being more resplendent than met his taste he expressed displeasure. My mother 'bridled' at this and without hesitation twitched it from around his neck and threw it on the fire, where it was quickly consumed. My grandmother and my mother saw to it that his body linen was changed frequently so that although he did not smell of aftershave his presence was not offensive.

The condition of his teeth left much to be desired. Some were missing but those which remained ranged from yellow to black, with here and there a greenish tinge. Whether he had bad breath was not easily discovered, for more often than not he smelled of ale. His nose was his most amazing feature. It was swollen and red and was of a kind described as a 'bottle-nose'. On it were protuberances of a whitish hue. When I questioned him about them he said that each one had cost him a lot of money to acquire, and that it was beyond the power of most people to gain them. He also volunteered the information that in his time he had drunk enough ale to float a battleship. My great-uncle also smoked 'twist' in a little short-stemmed clay pipe, which was blackened with use.

To sum up he looked part scoundrel, part vagrant and swashbuckler and in another age would have passed for a pirate. Undoubtedly he was to some degree selfish and self-centred as bachelors tend to be. He was a parasite inasmuch as he had settled on his sister, my grandmother, with presumably the tacit consent of my grandfather.

I have since learnt that my grandparents had cause to be grateful to my great-uncle, who was not such a parasite after all. It was he who had paid the rent it seemed, when they lived at Model Cottage and were obviously in need of assistance. No doubt there were other occasions, possibly many, when he had helped out. These were things which even my sharp little ears failed to catch.

Neverthless, it was a curious relationship and it intrigued me in trying to assess it. There was no doubt at all that we had a great affection for him, and he for us.

As for myself, I was protected and enfolded by love, for they all loved me in their own ways. They were kind, solicitous for my welfare and as far as they could be, generous. Each member had a highly developed individuality, often bordering on the eccentric. I grew up surrounded by wit, wisdom and a good deal of laughter.

The Characters Emerge

There was, however, something which was beginning to emerge and which would soon have to be revealed. Up to now I had looked upon my grandfather and grandmother as my parents, although they were much older than those of my school fellows. My mother I still recognised as a very much older sister and my Uncle Ben was my brother. As for my great-uncle, he was my uncle.

From conversations not meant for me and hints dropped at school I began to suspect that my position in the family unit was not a normal one.

A Disturbing Revelation

THE Village of my birth is Hambleton in the Fylde area of Lancashire. It lies about equidistant from Blackpool and Fleetwood on the River Wyre, a tidal river with its estuary at Fleetwood. To approach Hambleton from the Blackpool side one has to cross Shard Bridge, which is a toll bridge. A few miles down the river a ferry boat plies between Fleetwood and Knott-End-on-Sea.

The isolation caused by the river to the villagers of Hambleton, Stalmine, Preesall and Knott-End had left time suspended for centuries. In my day manners and customs and general mode of life were jealously preserved, scarred a little maybe for the moment by the enlightenment of lads of the village who had been forced to travel beyond the confines of their village boundaries and whose eyes had been opened wide by the horrifying experience of war.

The bonds were strong, and could be traced backwards for generations. The family whose name I had taken and in which I had half a share was such a one. Different families had intermarried, and the characteristics of each were much discussed in farmhouse and in cottage.

One season moved into another, the land continued to produce its cycle of crops, the hedgerows came alive, then slept. It was as if the inhabitants were anaesthetised into a kind of lethargy, lulled into tranquil acceptance by the gentle rhythms of the changing seasons, the mesmeric effect of the slow, steady repetitions of seed-times and harvests. Physically very active, they were still content to remain splendidly isolated, indeed desired it, with no wish to step beyond the limits of this serene outpost of Arcady.

Hambleton Village, about 1939.

I myself was an Arcadian, metaphorically playing on my pipe throughout the live-long day, whilst sheep grazed undisturbed about me. Ambition played little if any part, and it was only when eventually I stepped outside the invisible fence and looked back on my comfortable enclosure that I became fully awake.

I was born at Model Cottage, a house which must have been at the edge of the village at that time. It was at the end of a very narrow lane which itself extended to a track leading to the fields beyond. My first recollection was of watching the ducks on the pond which was within yards of the house, as I sat propped up in a high perambulator.

Quite soon afterwards we moved a couple of miles away to a tiny cottage, one of a row of three joined together, near Jolly's Farm in Out Rawcliffe. They were of the one up, one down type, with very low ceilings and oak beams, and must have been very old. They have long since been demolished.

It was here that I suffered from bad bouts of croup, "a severe disease in the throats of children, accompanied by a hoarse cough". A bad attack could result in asphyxiation. I was bundled downstairs in the middle of the night, wrapped in a blanket. Mother would nurse me whilst my grandmother plied me with spoonsful of hot bacon fat heated in a frying pan. Croup granules kept in small glass phials were also said to be efficacious.

It may have been that this recurring malady which caused discomfort in my early years gave my family the idea that I had a weak chest, or it may have been my doctor who was himself very wheezy and running to fat. I was afraid of this doctor. When he visited me at the cottage I evaded him by running upstairs and crawling under the bed in the same manner in which a cat does when it wants to hide. He followed me upstairs and with much puffing and panting poked me out, at the same time telling me in a low voice which did not carry downstairs that I was "an awkward little bugger".

Every year, come the approach of winter a large wad of cotton-wool, orange-coloured and impregnated with a substance which gave off a strong distinctive odour was pinned with large safety-pins on to my vest or liberty-bodice. It stretched across my chest and was hot and itchy. The trade name of this product was Thermogene. Whoever sat next to me at school would surely benefit from the vapours with which I was surrounded, unless that person was also carrying a similar covering on his chest, or upon the as yet undeveloped bosom.

In spring a small piece of wool was removed every week, so that by mid-summer with a bit of luck I would be free for two or three months. As I grew older I took it off altogether and hid it, only replacing it at crucial times like bath-nights when my under-linen would be changed and all would be revealed. By the time I was about eight there was no more talk of Thermogene. Whether it did indeed save my life, whether I did have a weak chest cannot now be assessed.

There was another infallible remedy for bad chests, never to my knowledge applied to me. It was drastic and needed some fortitude both on the part of the administrator and the recipient. Goose-grease, mixed with whisky if a particularly keen bite was desired, was rubbed briskly and unstintingly into the chest wall. From this admixture there arose an interesting aroma which tended to fill the room in which the patient lodged. A stiff covering of brown paper sealed the application and crackled alarmingly with every movement. The pores were opened to such an extent that when the paper was removed the patient could not venture out for a few days, or dreadful infections of the lungs were apt to occur, thus defeating the object of the original treatment. Most families kept goose-grease along with their senna-pods, Cascara, Carter's Little Liver Pills, Sloane's Liniment and in my case, croup granules.

In this cottage I carried out my own private execution, young as I was. Having heard my elders recount with some relish the hanging of a felon, I took my stuffed toy, which was called 'Sunny Jim', attached him by the neck with string to a hook which was already in a beam in the ceiling, and hung on to his heels until he was dead. From that time onwards his head listed to one side in a disconsolate manner. Sunny Jim had been a quaint-looking creature before his maltreatment. He had come to me by collecting a number of vouchers issued by the manufacturers of a well-known breakfast product called 'Force', and had a curious appendage like a pig-tail at the back of his head. Although he was not a coloured gentleman his dress was more suitable for a negro minstrel. My grandmother who was my supervisor, had been standing at the door chatting to the lady who lived in the next cottage. When she came in she was taken aback at my act and reproved me very forcefully with her tongue.

It was only fitting that my grandfather should have a grandfather clock. This he valued above all other domestic possessions. On a Saturday afternoon, two or three times a year, he would oil its mechanism, using a feather. The cord would become frayed and he would spend time fitting a new one, sometimes showing frustration when he couldn't manipulate it on to the pulleys. One dark evening when I was

17

about five, our women-folk were out, possibly gossiping at the farm next door or at some function or other. My grandfather, tired as he must have been, played hide and seek with me. He went so far as to open the door in his beloved clock and inserted his head and shoulders, making sure that he was not too hard to find. When we two had made our way to bed up the narrow stair I was allowed to creep in beside him as a special treat. As I clung close to his back for warmth he said we should think of and be sorry for people that night who were worse off than ourselves and who were homeless, and had no warm beds to lie in. He asked me quietly whether I would think of him "when he was dead and gone".

In the bedroom in which we lay was a framed text:

> *"A good name is rather to be chosen than great*
> *riches;*
> *and loving favour rather than silver and gold".*

When I was about seven we moved all our goods from Out Rawcliffe back to Hambleton. Everything was transported on a farm-lorry, horse-drawn of course, and driven by my Great-uncle Dick who has more than a mention soon. The journey was a memorable one for me as well as for everyone else. It was as if I had developed diarrhoea for the sole purpose of causing harassment. From time to time we were brought to a halt whilst I was lifted down to relieve myself on the wide grassy verge. What with croup, diarrhoea and the revelation of sadistic tendencies shown in my venture with 'Sunny Jim'. I promised to be quite a handful.

We alighted eventually at Crooklands Cottage, which, when approached from Ryecroft Corner is situated up a narrow lane which juts off left at the top of the Village. We had almost arrived back at the same spot from where we started, for a hundred yards or so further on was Model Cottage. We were to stay at Crooklands Cottage until I was sixteen or seventeen.

There was a substantial yard as well as a good sized kitchen garden, with two or three apple-trees and a few damson-trees. We stored coal in a small brick building which had been a pig-sty.

The one living room or kitchen was approached via the back door through a back-kitchen where the stone sink was. A roomy pantry complete with stone slabs was through a door on the left. Up the open stairs from the living room there were two bedrooms. The smaller of these had a ginnel or narrow passage-like extention which could hold a single bed at a pinch. Compared to our cramped quarters in Out Rawcliffe we now found ourselves in positive luxury.

There was no bathroom or hot water. The earth closet, a wooden structure of familiar traditional shape was housed in the yard, at least fifteen yards from the back door. As there was no lavatory indoors, visits to this place were perilous expeditions on dark, rainy nights with the wind howling in from the west. We had an ancient lantern battered by its long service. It lived in the back-kitchen and was candle-powered. Even accompanied by this veteran I had to have further moral support from another candle placed in the little window in the back-kitchen, where I could see it from where I sat with the door open. Needless to say, these missions were accomplished with all due speed, and it is a wonder that I did not suffer permanent internal damage as a result. I was not very brave I confess, but there was a reason for my timidity which I shall reveal in due course.

One of the pieces of furniture in our living-room was a sofa, forerunner of the settee. I found it hard to believe that these two ageing men, my grandfather and my great-uncle, sitting together on the sofa on a Sunday, making desultory conversation as they waited for the main meal of the week, had ever been young.

The starched damask tablecloth gleamed snow-white, the cutlery was laid and there was much activity ovenwards. There this ill-assorted pair sat smoking, my great-uncle with his evil-looking blackened short clay pipe, my grandfather with his briar. Wisps of grey smoke rose upwards. Had they really danced the nights away through the latter days of Queen Victoria's golden reign and through the short high summer of King Edward, which lasted a brief period from 1901 to 1910? Yet it was so.

Dressed in the height of contemporary fashion and wearing white gloves lest they should soil the ladies' dresses, they had whirled their partners round in Hambleton Reading Room. My grandmother had been amongst them, a buxon young woman then, her long skirts swirling outwards as she lent back in strong arms and was swirled round and round in the Old-fashioned Waltz. They would take their places in sets of Lancers or perform the nimble steps of the Polka.

There was an elegance in their bearing; a skill in their performance. Good manners prevailed and with them a gentlemanly consideration for women. To some extent, such qualities were retained into my adolescence a quarter of a century later, but already the decline was evident in comparison. There was an ever-increasing relinquishment of old-time standards until today such behaviour would evoke derision, and is to be observed only in tea-dances; those sad gatherings at which some senior citizens re-live their golden years.

With the exuberance of the young, with scant thought for the exacting day's toil ahead they danced into the early hours with the dawn drawing nearer. They also unwittingly were moving rapidly out of a period of peaceful respite into one of terrible slaughter. Within half-a-dozen years there would be empty places, ladies suddenly without their partners, for the youth and the not-so-youthful would have found their last resting places on the battlefields of Flanders.

My grandfather had actually played in an instrumental group called Bowmans' String Band. As intimated previously, my grandfather had an artistic temperament. This displayed itself in other members of his family and was to be carried into subsequent generations. The cello, my grandfather's instrument, hung in an honoured place on the wall beside his beloved clock. It was a treasured memorial to a previous age. Though he was never known to take it down and play it in his later years, I choose to think that he might have done so, had he lived a year or two longer when I would have become sufficiently proficient on the piano. Great-uncle Dick, my grandfather's brother, was versatile not only on the violin but also on tin-whistle and concertina. My Uncle Ben assures me that the concertina, which now rests in wistful retirement on top of a cupboard in his kitchen, is still in good working order. Bill Parkinson from Staynall and my grandfather's cousin, Joseph Breckall, also played violins. Stanley, my grandfather's nephew, completed the quintet, giving added harmonic richness on the piano.

The group did not restrict itself solely to local functions. A story is told of how its members trudged through the snow across the bleak, exposed Rawcliffe Moss as far afield as Garstang, a round trip of eighteen miles; and how my grandfather carried his cello, carefully encased in sacking to protect it from the weather, on his back.

History was to repeat itself two generations later, for I also became a member of a dance band, performing on that very same stage where those other Bowmans had sat and played all those years ago. It was I who now gyrated, careless for the morrow which was well able to take care of itself, on that same dance floor in the same big room, unchanged even to the pictures on the walls.

There was one big difference. Our band did not walk to engagements in other parishes. We were transported in Jimmy Bleasdale's car or van. It would have been difficult if not impossible for Arthur the drummer, to have clattered along with all the percussive devices contained in his drum-kit.

At the beginning of the Great War my mother was eighteen. On group photos taken when she was a girl, she appears as sensitive and modest, seemingly somewhat perplexed at her surroundings. This intensity and perplexity may have been partially due to the fact that she was short-sighted, a condition which was not discovered until her early teens. An attempt was made to rectify this deficiency, but I suspect that considerable damage had already been done, for she was to suffer with her eye-sight for the rest of her life. When she was fitted with her first spectacles she began to live in a miraculous new world with sunlight glinting on tiny pebbles and stalks of grass and delicately-tinted petals of flowers among which tiny creatures, hitherto unknown to her, flew or ran about.

An interesting feature of her childhood was that the summers were long, dry and hot. She seemed to have played in perpetual sunshine with her cousin Mary and their dolls. I was never convinced of this and had many arguments, some of them quite heated, on the subject. I would point out rather pompously that because this period had probably been the happiest of her life, she was wont to look upon it through rose-coloured spectacles. She lived to hear me eat my words. I became converted finally, for it has been verified that the seasons have indeed changed.

At school my mother was a keen, willing and able pupil, although she must have missed much which was written upon the blackboard. Not only had she a special attraction to poetry, she also had a strong constitution. I value greatly a splendid, though slightly battered leather-bound volume of Wordsworth's Poetical Works awarded as a special Prize for Attendance at Christmas 1906, when she was just turned eleven. It was presented by Mrs. T. Battersby at Hambleton Council School. The Headmaster was Mr. T. Martin, a formidable gentleman whose name is still mentioned with awe by those former pupils who survive. How, one wonders, would such a challenging choice as Wordsworth's poems be received by eleven-year-olds today; and what would now be considered a characteristic stimulant to the mind. My mother could quote whole stretches from established poets of the nineteenth century, learnt by heart at school and at home.

When she left school she worked as a day-girl in the dairy at a farm owned by the well-to-do Lewtas family, where she

Dominance prevails in garden of Hambleton School, circa 1907. My mother is the first girl from the left, facing camera.

helped to make butter and cheese. Later she was fortunate to gain what was thought to be a more prestigious post as parlour-maid to the Rev. Schofield, incumbent of the Parish of Stalmine. Curiously enough, his vicarage was in the Parish of Preesall. The good name of my mother's parents must have influenced her appointment.

As one can imagine, for it always happens in war-time, there was an increased interest shown by servicemen in eligible young ladies. My mother attracted her share of suitors and showed a healthy response in return. One photograph of her, taken when she was a comely young woman of twenty-two, is labelled in her own handwriting. Stalmine Vicarage, Preesall. Blighty 27.1.18, and bears the message 'Love and good wishes, From Alice XX'. I conclude that it was returned to her because yet another young fellow had 'gone west'. There is another photograph showing a presentable young soldier about my mother's age. It bears the name 'Ike'. Who was Ike I wonder, and whatever happened to him? Only when my mother had become old did she start to tell me about these years in detail, and I regret that I failed to record her revelations.

My Mother, when she worked at Stalmine Vicarage during the Great War, circa 1916.

A Disturbing Revelation

The name of one of these followers I did know quite early in my life. I suppose I had to be told, for it turned out that he was my father. When my mother and I were out walking on a Sunday evening in summer when I was about eleven, she plucked up the courage to tell me that she was my real mother, and that my real father was very much alive, although he had no power to interfere in my up-bringing. As I had already some idea of the true situation I did not feel much different, although I did find it difficult to call her mother.

This absentee father of mine had shown a restless spirit in childhood and adolescence. He was four years younger than my mother. When he was sixteen he ran away and 'joined up', giving a false age. He was a gunner in the Royal Field Artillery and by all accounts had been at the Battle of the Somme.

I was born on St. Patrick's Day, 1920, which is on the 17th March. This date was not inappropriate for a quarter of me was Irish. My mother had been very successful in keeping her condition hidden from everyone. Not even her own mother had suspected until the birth had actually taken place in her own home. My Uncle Ben who was hovering about at the time, then a lad of twelve, confirms that my entry was totally unheralded and struck like a thunder-bolt. I doubt whether I was considered to be important enough for such dramatic effects as shafts of lightning, but there was a storm blowing. My first cry, like the wail of a banshee, was heard in the early hours of the morning, when spirits are known to be at their lowest ebb.

One can only imagine the tragic look on my grandfather's face, the hurt which my grandmother felt when their only daughter, so modest and respectable, had given in to temptation and had let them down so badly by presenting them with their first grandchild, out of wedlock.

Whatever their feelings, they overcame them. To their lasting credit they accepted the responsibility of both mother and child. There was never any question of turning us out; we were at home, part of the family. The other partner responsible for my existence was as ignorant as anyone else of my anticipated arrival. By this time he had signed on for a further four years and had been sent to India.

My mother's plight left her remorseful and embittered. The greatest possession of my grandparents, family pride, had been struck a mighty blow. Yet to me there is an endearing side. It is, after all, a tale of young lovers, both overwhelmingly attracted to each other and vigorous in the fulfilment of their love. I was born of love and I am proud of it.

The tension of the Great War had not yet subsided. For the one it was miraculous to be alive and unscathed and to receive such comfort. For the other, compassion as well as sexual attraction must have played its part. They were both swept along on a strong emotional current to a climax which was inevitable.

Supernatural Diversion

IT is the winter evenings which stand out most in my memory at Crooklands Cottage, up to the time when I was becoming less dependant on others. The summer evenings were spent running about, playing hide-and-seek or rounders until my little friends and I were lathered in sweat.

After tea, when the table had been cleared and my grandfather was settled in his rocking chair over in the corner on the right of the fireplace, the hearth was cleared for the next operation. I was undressed, washed and put into my sleeping-suit. All this was carried out in front of the fire, where my night clothes had been put to warm previously. Two or three times a week a tin bath would be brought in and dumped on the hearth. There was a good deal of banging, a lot of obstacles to overcome on its journey from its hook in the cobbled yard by the back door through the narrow back kitchen.

The bath was filled with hot water and I was commanded to step in. If my mother was in charge I would have a rough ride, for in her zeal she tended to overdo things. The water would be just that degree too hot to be bearable and I would spring back with a cry after trying it with my toe. If I did get a reprieve by having a drop or two of cold water added very grudgingly, there would be no further concessions. She would gouge into my ears and rub furiously at my hair as if she were scrubbing a flagged floor. After she had dried me with a big towel, warmed ready, it was wonder that I had any skin left on my back.

27

WHEN EVERY DAY WAS SUMMER

This pursuit of cleanliness was worth it even if it was not fully appreciated by me, for I was allowed to creep on to my grandfather's knee and snuggle up against his waistcoat. He would put on his reading glasses and we would proceed to go through our nursery rhyme repertoire. The book we used was made of a linen material and had illustrations.

There was Goosey-Goosey-Gander who wandered up-stairs and downstairs and 'in my lady's chamber'. The only chamber I knew was the one my grandmother carried downstairs and emptied each morning. After rinsing it out with boiling water she would put it somewhere out of sight in the open air to 'sweeten'. How could a large bird like a gander roam about in a chamberpot? Was it a very large chamberpot or was the gander a gosling, new hatched? My query had to be explained. Again, there was Little Miss Muffet. The big black spider which sat by her did not bother me much. I was too concerned at the curious attraction which Miss Muffet had for 'curds and whey'. I knew what both products were, for I had been shown them resting in their great containers in dairies on their way to becoming cheese. Not only had the appearance put me off, but so had the sour smell of curdled milk which rose from the vats. Maybe this is why I cannot bear yogurt.

Buttermilk was a drink favoured by many but certainly never by me. It was the surplus liquid drawn off when butter was being made and had a rich, yellowish appearance. It was probably very nutritious. My great-uncle liked it, but I refused to touch it. It was the same with 'beest custard'. A custard pie made from 'beest' was considered a delicacy. 'Beestings' was the first milk drawn off a cow after calving, but with us it was shortened to 'beest'.

My grandfather and I continued, the one teaching patiently, the other learning. We went through letters, to words, to sentences and sometimes changed to numbers. At times he would introduce the verse of a hymn or some Christian instruction. He was very fond of analogies relating to sheep so we would go through 'Loving Shepherd of Thy Sheep' or 'The Lord's My Shepherd'.

Another favourite of his was 'There's a friend for little children, above the clear blue sky . . .' Was it, I have wondered, a cry from the heart. He was wise, my grandfather and would have assessed, looking back on his own life that I would need every bit of support I could get, more so because of the circumstances of my birth. He would foresee the fight that lay ahead for me.

"Honour thy father and thy mother, that thy days may be long in the land which the Lord thy God giveth thee". My grandfather would quote this text and go on to tell me that I should respect and should be good mannered to people older than myself. I must always raise my cap to my elders and pass the time of day. So it was that with loving insistence I was taught good manners in my own home.

The rules relating to my bedtime were fluid, depending on whether or not there was school the next day. I might be allowed to wait up for my great-uncle's return from the public house. His arrival was announced by the sound of his clogs on the cobbled path and soon on the flagged floor of the back kitchen. He would come in, blinking at the lamplight and bringing with him a whiff of the cold wintry air mingled with beer fumes. He breathed heavily from the exertions of his long walk and his alcoholic intake. When he had lowered himself ponderously into an old armchair placed at the opposite side of the fireplace to my grandfather, puffing monstrously, with his face congested and his white spots showing in great contrast on his glowing, purple nose, my task would be to unlace his clogs and take them off. My attentions saved him from having to lean forward and lessened the risk of his bursting a blood vessel. As it was his custom to place a bed of straw in each clog for warmth and for greater comfort, and as this had caused his feet to sweat, a rich, farmyard odour would rise to meet me. I was not repelled by it. After all, I was a child of the countryside and I passed shippons, pig-sties, stables and middens every day of my life. Moreover, I received a penny for carrying out my duty.

There was constant running battle between my great-uncle and the two women. My mother and grandmother resented his lack of hygiene, the farmyard smell and the bits of straw which sometimes fell on to the rug. They were shrill in their protests but he responded by closing one eye, turning his head sideways and saying nothing. This was a characteristic gesture he used to show his contempt for what he thought were trivialities invented by womenfolk, and was always followed by louder prolonged outbursts against him, which I think he invited for his inner enjoyment. My grandfather sitting opposite, remained neutral, said nothing, but might offer the trace of a smile when his wife was showing more than usual artistry in her expressions.

It will not have escaped the notice of readers, from what I have written so far, that there were certain currents of eccentricity present within the household. I grew up in an atmosphere in which people did not subscribe to an idea because it was the fashion to do so, or because most other people accepted it. My great-uncle usually lent the other way. As a matter of principle, if the rest of the world stood out for one thing he would take the opinion which was directly opposed to it. I learnt that there were at least two view-points if not more to be considered. I did not realise as I grew up how much I was being influenced by this individualism, this independence of thought. I found that I became more interested in individual skills and could stand a good deal of my own company.

I would have welcomed a companion, however, when I climbed the stairs on my way to bed with my candle which guttered in the down-draught. My thoughts were centred on the supernatural, which was also the cause of my lightning visits to the lavatory.

When the wind howled in the chimney, when the paraffin lamp was lower than usual and was creating darker shadows and when the fire had burnt low, the conversation turned to ghosts. The northern word for ghost is 'boggart'. I have never known such a family as ours when it came to boggarts. When I mentioned the tales to my schoolmates, the tales I had heard told round the fire, most of them knew little or nothing about them and were not at all interested. I was asked by sceptics whether I had seen any 'boggart muck'. Only the physical proof present in a trail of boggart droppings would confirm the existence of boggarts.

My elders continued to tell and re-tell their stories, seemingly unaware that they had a very imaginative, impressionable petrified child in their midst.

By the side of the school playground there is a lane which runs at right-angles to Church Lane and joins it by the school gates. When I was a boy it was called 'Old Arthur's Lane'. There is a hill falling to Church Lane which my grandfather would have called 'broo'. The lane bears no resemblance to what it once was. Then it was narrow and dark with tall hawthorn hedges overhanging on either side. Now it is wide and light with no hedge at all where a housing estate replaces Catteralls' pastures.

Down this broo would come a procession of six men, walking with great solemnity of bearing. They were carrying a coffin. As the churchyard was just around the corner there was nothing unusual in a funeral. Most people were carried shoulder-high to their burial. But wait. On closer inspection the bearers were all without heads. Furthermore, this melancholy group would materialise from nowhere and would vanish just as quickly.

Having just experienced this manifestation one might be fortunate enough (or unfortunate, according to one's attitude to the supernatural), to witness another performance. A glance over the shoulder would take in a stile at the top of a raised bank on the opposite side of the road to the schoolhouse. If a figure were silhouetted against the stile in the moonlight, it would be the troubled spirit of a policeman who had cut his throat, a grisly reminder from the past.

The churchyard itself was such an obvious place for sightings that more often than not it was overlooked. If a tiny lamp were to be seen flickering its way up the path it might be a restless inmate or it might be the light from Aunty Mary's lantern. From her appearance she was my aunt removed by three or four generations for she was a little shrivelled up walnut of a lady, very old and stooped. I have since discovered that this aged lady of my childhood was none other than my grandfather's sister; that once upon a time she had been pretty enough to attract a husband, a Mr. Bramwell who was a game-keeper; and that between them they had produced two off-spring. Tragedy had struck Aunt Mary at least once, as it had the unfortunate Mr. Bramwell. He had met a quite unforeseen and untimely end when he was run over by a train at Carnforth. The story goes that he was on his way back from buying a neck-tie to be worn at a 'rent dinner', an important social event, when his overcoat had blown over his head and the train had struck him.

My grandmother was very fond of Aunt Mary, and never missing an opporunity for gossip, would call in for a chat. Aunt Mary lived alone in a little dream cottage past Church Lane going up towards Cutts Lane and Rawcliffe. Only a stone's throw away was Moss Side Farm, where my great-grandfather, her father had farmed, and where presumably she had spent her own childhood. The cottage was white-washed, thatched and there were roses round the door. Inside was low, dark and cosy with lots of rugs, cushions and anti-macassars. The fire was always nicely 'gleed' with coals showing red and the kettle on the hob, just boiled. A little painted tin would be taken down from the mantel-piece with its draped surround and I would be offered a couple of biscuits. There was always one with pink icing, or failing that, one with a coating of sugar.

I nibbled and licked at my biscuit, taking care not to drop crumbs on Aunt Mary's peg rug, and leant against the comfort and protection of my grandmother's knee as she sat in the ingle nook. I observed Aunt Mary who sat opposite, leaning forward to seek the warmth of her fire, which she tended with such care, as the two of them sipped their tea which was indispensable support for their social exchanges. All female relatives and associates of my mother and grandmother, these latter two particularly, were addicted to this beverage and drank cup after cup as they talked yet again of events which had happened long before I was born; of people who were now only names on headstones in Hambleton churchyard. I could not for the life of me comprehend that Aunt Mary had ever been other than very old and frail. There must have been a lot of tenacity and spirit left in her though, and a sinewy strength, characteristic of old ladies who have weathered storms and turbulence successfully, whose physical frames have been reduced through the years, so that they still hop about like birds, their eyes still bright and alert, missing nothing.

Come to think of it, there may have been another reason for Aunt Mary's resilience, and that tea was not her only means of comfort and sustenance. Occasionally Aunt Mary would produce small, delicate wine glasses for my grandmother and herself, from her corner cupboard which reposed in the mellow dimness of her cosy living room, and would fill them with libations of elderberry wine — home brewed. Elderberry bushes grew in profusion, bearing flowers and berries for all to pick. The amber liquid, so innocuously-sounding, I found when I was older had the kick of a mule if it was mature, as hers would be. Could it be that these ladies, so proper in deportment, so refined in bearing with never a hint at innuendo or impropriety, may well have had their vigour and pertness sustained by the contents of Aunt Mary's cellar?

Aunt Mary was in charge of the heating at the church. On Friday and Saturday nights and at other times when it was necessary throughout the winter months, she had to turn out to light and to stoke the small boiler so that the church would be warm for the congregation. When it was very frosty she made two trips, the second one in the early morning. This meant that she walked a distance of about three miles. Her bent figure under its cloak and shawl would make its way very, very slowly up the churchyard path, the little light bobbing as it went.

She had to go round the back of the church and descend some awkward stone steps into the boiler house which

33

itself was like a tomb. Surrounded by her encampment of corpses, many of whom she would have known when they were boys and girls, she was very vulnerable and could have been attacked and murdered without any hindrance, for no one was there to hear except possibly, the schoolmaster in his bed nearby. As it was, Aunt Mary survived to die peacefully in her own bed and was put to rest in the place where she had given devoted service.

* * * *

Junctions and crossroads were favourite spots for boggarts. It was as if such situations had chosen to give maximum effect from all sides. My Great-uncle Dick (Richard, my grandfather's brother) was probably the doyen of Hambleton ghost-spotters. In fact, his fame may have extended to cover the whole Fylde. He it was who had seen the Bickerstaff Boggart several times, usually in a most eerie lane set between silent, menacing woods. I must confess that this fringe of Hambleton has always been to me an ominous, brooding place even in broad daylight, although I have never actually seen anything unusual, save for the absence of human activity, in spite of the fact that people live in the area.

Our village was encircled by boggarts whose positions had been as carefully chosen as if a military commander had been in charge. Having run the gauntlet to outlying villages one could not gain any respite, for they had their own resident ghosts.

When I was older the homeward journey made in the dark on my bicycle from Land Hill Farm, an isolated homestead in lonely, open country some way from the Village, were always challenges to the supernatural. Whichever way I chose there were boggarts. If I turned left there was the Pig-tail Boggart, and further on, the Carr Lane Cat. A right turn meant Bickerstaff and the churchyard. They say that the pulse-rate should be accelerated at least once a day. Fear, and treading vigorously on the pedals did it for me.

My grandfather was once approached by an acquaintance, who revealed to him in trembling tones that he had
seen 'Th'Owd Lad' in a field by Hambleton Church. As
Th'Owd Lad was none other than the Devil himself the
acquaintance had cause to be timorous. "Tha looks frick-
ened to dee-ath. Tha musta sin Th'Owd Lad", might well
have been my grandfather's comment.

My grandfather, acting in a neighbourly fashion into
which some curiosity intruded, set off towards the churchyard, companion in reluctant attendance, to confront the
Devil. He must have felt sufficiently secure in his own
purity to come near such a formidable adversary, though
being indoctrinated with Holy Writ he would have been the
first to admit that no-one was entirely without sin. Who
better than my grandfather for such an errand. Not only
was he cleansed spiritually week by week; he also sent
paeans of praise skywards to the Seat of Judgement. He
above all could surely claim maximum protection, being
one of the privileged few.

Picture these two natives of the village then, approaching the spot specially chosen by the Devil. Peering through
the gloom, for all unearthly visitors chose a bad light, and
the Devil, in spite of his awesome presence was no excep-
tion, the outline of a low hedge could just be made out, and
behind it a menacing, elongated shaggy face topped by two
horns. At this moment my grandfather may have wished to
turn and run, but if there was one thing he did not lack it
was courage. He had sensed that something was not quite
right, for did not the Devil have two tight outcrops of horn
set well forward, whilst here were great big ones with wide
curves. He took a step or two forward to get a better look
and saw a cow or bullock of a breed never before seen in
Hambleton. A local farmer, less conservative than the rest,
with a view to greater profit, had imported some Hereford
cattle of which this beast was one. Another mystery was
solved to the immense relief of one possibly and some
disappointment on the part of the other.

My great-uncle in his nocturnal visits to 'Wardleys', the

Wardleys Hotel overlooking the River Wyre, a distance of about a mile from our house, had to cross a little bridge called the 'Clough' or 'Clow' which crossed a tiny tributary. Behold, the 'Clow Boggart' had its post there. The risk of experiencing a visitation was obviously negligible to my great-uncle when his ale was at stake, for he kept going. On his way home had he been accosted, he would have paused, closed one eye, turned his head to one side and told it to 'bugger off'.

Yet taciturn and phlegmatic though he was on such matters, he himself confessed that something inexplicable had happened to him. It was when he was a young man, working at Mains Hall, across the river beyond Shard Bridge. Going up the wide stairway of the house with no one else near, he sensed that a person invisible to him had passed him by. There was the unmistakable swish of a lady's petticoats and long skirts. It had made him feel "queer".

In this very kitchen where I now sat listening, my grandmother when a little girl (for she had lived in this same cottage long ago), had happened to look up the stairs and had seen a little wrinkled old woman peering down at her. She seemed to bow or to bend forward — then she vanished. After my grandmother had told me this, my eyes had a habit of drifting to those stairs, half expecting to see what she had seen. To this day I am aware of the unknown at the top of the stairs.

It goes without saying that we in our own little cottage had our own unearthly resident. When all was still its heavy measured footsteps would be heard coming round the side of the house. We knew they would never arrive. At first someone or other, never my grandfather, would rush out to try to identify the intruder, but there was never anything to see. My great-uncle, whose bedroom faced the back was not easily stirred from his bed. Yet once he did get up to fling open the window and to shout a warning to whoever was there. The light of a full moon illuminated the cobbled path but there was no one.

Supernatural Diversion

My mother, never one for rushing to bed, would stay up late smoothing or, to use a more modern term, ironing. When all the house was still she was rudely disturbed by the sounds like a barrow full of gravel being tipped. They came from under the floor by the front door which was seldom used. Very suddenly she stopped her smoothing and beat a hasty retreat to bed.

My grandmother became very nervous about staying on her own in the evenings. When I was older and began to visit friends for an hour or two she was always eager to see me return.

I do not know whether it was an over active imagination or conditioning, or whether there was a psychic strain inherited from some branch of the family, but supernatural phenomena travelled with us to our next house, when I was older. There were a couple of disturbing manifestations, one of them recurring, of which I never found a satisfying explanation.

Looking ahead to when I was seventeen or eighteen, I would be lying in bed in this other house, tired after a hard day's work in the fields, when I would be aware of sibilant whispers, or voices talking against each other in undertones. They seemed to come from the living-room immediately below my bedroom. I formed a mental picture of a group of old crones gathered close round the fire, engaged in agitated, malicious gossip. I heard them not once but several times. Years later, after I was married, my young wife and I occupied the same room for a time. When I happened by chance to mention the noises to her she confessed that she had heard them and had been puzzled. She had thought at first that birds had been trapped in the old chimney.

In that same room one summer's night we both became suddenly wide awake. In the unnatural stillness we heard the old fashioned 'sneck' or door fastening lift as if someone was about to enter. A tremor went right through me and my hairs on the back of my head lifted. I got up, reluctantly I admit, padded across the room and flung open the door.

WHEN EVERY DAY WAS SUMMER

There was nothing on the other side, or down the stairs or anywhere in the house.

Some people reject utterly the subject of ghosts, some retain an open mind, or so they say; others not only accept but show enthusiasm for exploration in this field. Whatever the answer, it did not relieve my problems when I was still very much in the short-trousers stage. Was there any wonder that my nocturnal visits to and from the lavatory were made with such trepidation and such haste; that my candle shook slightly sometimes as I climbed the stairs; that my senses were alive to the slightest sound as I lay huddled up with the bed clothes pulled over my head and the night light still burning?

A Confession of Practical Inadequacy

I DO not suppose that if I were to go into the Infants' Class at Hambleton Council School I would notice very much difference from when I was there sixty years ago. The posters will have changed, as will the great shiny map of the world dominating one wall, with large expanses of red which marked the realms of the British Empire. Otherwise the atmosphere will be much the same.

At five years old I was dragged to school for the first time. There will still be children screaming and clutching as they are held tightly by embarrassed mothers, who on such occasions wish their off-spring to vaporise. It was my grandmother who had the unenviable task of marching me down the long country lanes from Rawcliffe for my first day at school. For a week until I settled down, I sailed along, held firmly by one hand, my feet hardly touching the ground, protesting most of the way. The nearer we got, the more clamorous were my protestations. There was no pleading when I arrived. I was met by Mrs. Youngs, bundled into the classroom and put in my place very firmly.

Up to now I had been so sheltered, and I seemed such a long way from home. Furthermore, it was too far for me to go home for lunch (or dinner as we country-folk called it), so I must have taken a bite to eat with me.

At the end of a day which seemed endless, I would rush out into the playground and meet my grandmother who would be waiting for me. She was easily recognised, for she wore a white bonnet, the flaps of which hung down to her shoulders.

Mrs. Youngs was one of the old type of teacher. I am happy to say that there are still some of her kind left, though one wonders for how long. She must have been in her sixties, with the end of her active life in view. Had she been beautiful in her youth? It was hard to think so, for she now had a long, melancholy face. My attention was drawn to her wrinkled jowls, not unlike those of my great-uncle but possibly more pendulous. In her eyes were compassion and understanding.

She wore woolly, tweedy clothes, woollen stockings and serviceable shoes. It is still the uniform of efficient, down-to-earth ladies of some breeding and refinement, living elegantly on modest means.

Her husband, Mr. Youngs, was the headmaster when I first started, but he was soon to withdraw through ill-health. He had fought as a non-commissioned officer in the Great War and it was known that he had a problem with drink. He gave his wife a lot of worry and sometimes the class was disrupted when she had to leave in a hurry.

Alcoholism was not uncommon, especially among ex-officers. There was at least one other so afflicted in our small community. It was sad but understandable. Responsibility beyond their years had been thrust upon these poor young men. They had been worked to the point of utter exhaustion under unbelievably terrible conditions. Their casualties had been enormous. Their consolation and survival had been in whisky, to which they had a greater access than the rank-and-file. Mr. Youngs in his better periods was both firm and efficient and could manage the most reluctant and unruly of his pupils.

We beginners sat two to our little desks, boys and girls mixed. At first we wrote on small trays with slate bottoms on to which were sprinkled layers of find sand. We formed our letters in the sand, using wooden skewers. When they had been checked and corrected we shook the trays and were ready to begin again. The next step was slates and slate pencils before we were considered good enough for pens and paper.

I cannot remember whether we actually did use ink in the infants' class. We might have been too young to be trusted with it. But when we did we used little ink-wells which slotted into circular apertures in the desks. The ink-wells were refilled by the ink monitor. The wooden pen-holders were fitted with detachable metal nibs. The bored or frustrated, and there were quite a few of these, could easily spoil their nibs by stabbing them in the wood of the desks. It was not entirely unknown for a nib to be projected into human flesh. Only the criminal types went in for that sort of thing for it was almost a capital offence.

Once my homesickness was over I was a ready pupil and found no difficulty in doing what was required. There were two occasions, however, when Mrs. Youngs treated me with disfavour. The first time it was my great-uncle's fault. He had taught me certain swear words, not very fearsome by modern standards, but enough to get my legs smacked forcibly when Mrs. Youngs heard me cursing another pupil. I was placed behind the blackboard in solitary confinement for what seemed a long, long time. It had its effect. I never forgot the ordeal, never swore again in Mrs. Youngs' presence or even in the playground.

In order to explain my other misdemeanours it must be said that I would go out of my way to avoid being trapped into undertaking what are known as creative skills; or to make or repair anything unless it involves the tools and implements used in gardening, where I am more at home than most.

I tried once, when I was married and should have known better, to make a garden frame out of wood. As it was raining I started my project in the cellar. Having put it together, working hastily with no finesse, I was called up for my tea. On my return I found it hard to believe that my structure which I had left so upright and proud, was now sitting in a dejected looking heap on the cellar floor. Not to be deterred I forced it together again, using six inch nails this time and causing splinters all over the place. I made sure that it would never collapse again. Then I found it wouldn't go through the cellar door. "Let wrath be unconfined". I took my sledge hammer to it and demolished it. Had Mrs. Youngs been about I should have spent eternity behind the blackboard.

I have met men who peer into the entrails of electrical gadgets, entranced, and solder tiny wires together. When I tried to make minor electrical repairs disaster struck. I plunged a large pair of ordinary pliers into a fuse-box and attacked the wires without bothering to switch off the power, and was flung right across the room, ending up quivering and in some disarray in the far corner. More violent curses followed, for I always put the blame on inanimate objects and never on me.

I mended a light switch in the kitchen, only to create another problem. The wire was old and corroded, so I cut off a bit at a time and chipped away at the wall, until finally I got everything working and set the switch in cement. It was only then that my wife, passing by, pointed out that the switch was no good for her, as it was so far up the wall towards the ceiling that it could only be operated by an eight-foot giant.

All this is relevant to my story, for my lack of manual dexterity led to my second misdemeanour in the infants' class.

Were I called upon to make a list of skills which I should least like to do, in order of preference, the one at the very bottom would be knitting, with the construction of cuddly toys just above it. It is ironic, therefore, that knitting, or rather my incompetence in it, led to my fall from grace.

The division of labour was kept strictly and preserved jealously, as it had been so since our ancestors lived in reed huts in the swamps. Just suppose for a moment that my grandfather had shown a sudden eagerness to knit. He would have been strongly discouraged by my grandmother. Had my grandmother tried to persuade him to knit he would have been most affronted.

A Confession of Practical Inadequacy

Who then had introduced this liberal idea where not only girls but boys were to be taught such a skill? Apparently there were trendy educationalists sixty years ago, when historically there shouldn't have been. It was with foreboding that I watched preparations for our assault upon domestic crafts. Even the grading of knitting needles seems wrong. The largest is 0 and they decrease in size as the numbers rise. Our needles were made of wood and there was no known grade. They were so big that they were off the chart. Some of the more frail children could not keep them in the required position for more than a few seconds at a time. The monitor giving them out almost collapsed under the weight of his burden.

Speaking from long experience, for I have seen it happen time and time again all my working life, a scheme is always planned in a certain way. The organisers work out the details with painstaking accuracy, then with great deliberation they reverse everything so that the greatest chaos is created. It is called retrograde action, and it never fails. A tiny example could be seen in choice of colour of our wool. Instead of a modest grey or brown which would not show dirt they had chosen snow white. Thus it was assured by perverse administrators sitting chuckling in the County Offices at Preston, that the greatest damage was done.

I tucked my enormous implements under my armpits and made a desperate attempt to shape the first loop, or, if you must have the technical name, to 'cast on'. I watched the progress of Hilda, the little girl who was soon to be my next door neighbour at Crooklands Cottage. Her work, performed with consummate skill, grew and grew until by the end of the session there was a large scarf about a foot wide which almost reached the floor. It fooled the planners by remaining in its pristine state of whiteness.

I did not need a Double First to reach the conclusion that Hilda could already knit. All the girls could knit, young as they were, and some of the boys were struggling valiantly with the wool and producing creditable results. I was out on a limb. My wool was so tangled round my uncontrollable

43

pit-props of needles that it became impossible to unravel without cutting bits off it. In addition, the more I grappled with it with my feverish, moist hands the dirtier it became. When the time came to put away the results of our endeavours mine resembled a smallish, brownish, furry animal which had been sleeping rough. To increase its suffering it had been impaled by two darts made by an amateur hunter before it had been put to sleep by the vet.

We were given large, white labels on which our names were written. We attached these before we put our work away in a large wicker linen-basket. I watched Hilda fold her creation and place it gently to rest. I stuffed mine in beside it and watched the lid close. I had already decided on a plan of action.

Right at the beginning of the next session there was an unpleasant scene. In my hands was placed a most complimentary effort which bore my name, whilst Hilda was given my failure, now bearing her name. I bent to my needles and watched her reaction under lowered lids.

For a moment or two she looked unbelievably at what she held. Then came a most harrowing cry which pierced everyone present. There followed floods of tears and my poor little animal figure was rejected and flung to the floor, falling heavily because of the 'darts'.

I tried to keep a low profile but it was to no avail. My sneaky, underhand trick was discovered, as I should have known it would be. Mrs. Youngs grilled me with such determination that I soon confessed, with tears on my part, that I had switched names.

What shame I suffered. Throughout every other knitting lesson I stood in 'solitary', removed from the guileless ones and hidden from view behind the largest blackboard. The playground saw me not for some time, for I was kept in at breaks and dinner times, only being allowed out to relieve myself.

There is a footnote to my unhappy story. No lasting harm was done to Hilda. She did not suffer nightmares or have convulsions on the classroom floor at the sight of me, or of a needle. Fortunately for her, there were no clinics to which she could be sent to have the incident magnified out of all proportion. Fortunately for me, there were no psychologists to probe into my behaviour patterns so that I would be disturbed for the rest of my life. Hilda bore me no grudge at all. She and her husband still send cards for my Irish birthday and at Christmas — all the way from Canada at that. Mrs. Youngs did not bear down on me and instil in me that I was a thoroughly bad lot. She never reflected on my disgrace once I had been punished. In a way I became a kind of Little Lord Fauntleroy, without the velvet trappings or the buckled shoes. I never stepped out of line; never was caned. I got on with my work in the classroom, longing for home time when I would be free to roam the Arcadian pastures and woods. With the three R's I was in my element. Reading was my delight and solace. Other subjects I tolerated, some I despised.

I do not think that I went out of my way to ingratiate myself with pupils or staff. My shyness and lack of confidence made me to some extent withdrawn if not at times aloof. Like lots of others, I probably disliked school more than I liked it. Schools are necessary inventions, I suppose, in our civilisation but they are artificial institutions neverthless.

For about six years, day in and day out in term time I attended my institution. So little impact had the period upon me in a social way, that at the end of it I scarcely remembered it at all.

Customs and
Classroom

DURING the 1920's conditions for most working-class families were thought to be very bad, and no doubt they were. But if the breath of financial scarcity and insecurity did brush our cheeks once in a while, it was as a reminder of rather than as a menace to survival. Where we lived in our country back-water remote from urbanization, not so much in miles as in slow communication and transport, it was a light breath in comparison to that which blew fiercely in the industrial areas of the North. One only needed to tour the under-privileged areas of Preston, some eighteen miles away to see sheer, stark poverty. My grandfather might visit Preston once a year on a Whit Monday to watch the procession; my grandmother never went when I knew her. What news filtered in was through newspapers and verbal exchanges, rather than from personal experience.

I never went to school barefoot. Neither, as far as I know (and I may be wrong), did any other child in my village in my era. There may have been a few worn soles which needed to be stuffed with cardboard or paper where boots were worn, but again, I never suffered such discomfort. There was probably a different tale to tell during the Great War.

We could also extend beyond the 'bread and dripping' diet which was traditional for those who lived near to starvation. The rest of the country would have been suffering indeed if we in the Fylde had gone short of fruit and vegetables. Most of the older cottages had kitchen gardens with fruit trees as well. There were even pigsties and room for poultry for the more ambitious who had a little capital for the initial outlay.

My grandfather, ageing as he was, and with his long working hours, still found time to sow and plant the large garden at Crooklands Cottage. My great-uncle helped. It was there that I learnt at first-hand the succession of vegetables, and even if I did not take the keen interest in

My Grandmother and Grandfather posed in front of the apple-tree in the garden at Crooklands Cottage.

gardening which I did later, I saw how each crop was grown. In the autumn the late potatoes were lifted and put in a 'hog'. The crop was placed in a big heap and and covered with straw before a roof of soil was heaped on to it to protect the contents from frost. It wasn't as simple as it sounds, for if the hog was prepared badly, the whole lot would rot. Our potatoes, grown to last us for much of the year, would have been ruined.

To a considerable extent we were self-supporting in vegetables. Fruit trees bore apples, both cooking and eating, damsons, Victoria plums and pears. We also had raspberries and gooseberries. It goes without saying that my mother and grandmother made jam. Our relatives who lived on farms sometimes brought butter and cheese, a cut off a side of fat bacon or a fowl. There was always something to eat if one lived amid the fruitful orchards and fertile fields. My counterparts in the back-to-backs of the big cities, breathing in the fog which was inescapable in the smoke-laden air, would have marvelled at my good fortune — or would they? Habit is hard to break, and given the choice they may have elected to keep to their own tiny, enclosed backyard and the filtered sunlight.

I suppose I must have worn the standard outfit throughout my school days at Hambleton. Boys wore short trousers of a strong serviceable material such as corduroy or whipcord. To have appeared in long trousers would have attracted ridicule from all sides. Yet the length of some of the short trousers varied as one can see from school photographs. There would always be two or three 'three-quarter lengths', usually 'hand-me-downs' to be seen in the school playground at any one time.

I wore a woollen jersey or gansy with buttons at the collar, and a straight knitted tie. Some of the boys from outlying farms wore coats which could have been their fathers' cast-offs. As the pockets were always stuffed to overflowing with bottling-string, staples, hen-rings and other flotsam of the farm, there was always a danger of being struck forcibly by them when the owner swung round in play.

There was an affectation for large cloth caps at this period. They sat flat on the head and overlapped for quite a distance on each side. They had enormous peaks.

In the days when one "watched the birdie" (and when the visit of the photographer to the village was an attraction in itself), there were seconds of strained silence and utter stillness before the photograph was taken. This is why those "having their likeness taken" look as if they are either drugged, or educationally sub-normal, or both. They stare at the camera with an intensity of expression which indicates difficulty with co-ordinated thought-processes. Under their mushroom hats they stand, I among them, perennially young.

Me, aged about eight. Note 'gansy' and knitted tie.

We either wore clogs or boots, the former being more customary in earlier days, the latter in later years. The sound of clog-irons rattling on the cobblestones of the mill towns of the North was reproduced in much smaller volume by children going to and from our school.

The girls wore print dresses in summer and either pinafore dresses or skirts and jumpers in winter. These did not always fit as well as they might, for they would have been passed down the line from one sister to another. Because

49

they were girls they managed to keep neater and cleaner than the boys.

Every morning I walked down the road from Crooklands Cottage across the farmyard to call for Harry Catterall who lived at Sunderlands Farm. There would be great bustle and activity, for milking-time was just finishing. All cows were milked by hand. I might see Willie Catterall who had served in the Great War. Willie was a much older brother to Harry. He was an expert on horses and if the stable door was open it was pretty certain that he was there. He always had a cheery greeting for me, as did all the Catterall family. When I gained a success or two they always expressed pleasure, which I felt was genuine.

I would pass through the dairy, having difficulty at times in avoiding buckets and milk-kits on my way. It was cold-looking with stone slabs and water always being splashed about. It was friendly and spotlessly clean and in the roomy kitchen there was always a fire. Often Mr. Catterall, a jolly Pickwickian figure, would give me an expansive greeting as he sat waiting for breakfast. On winter mornings Harry would be buttoned into a pair of long leggings made of leather. Mrs. Catterall, a kindly, matronly figure, used a button-hook which intrigued me. I never liked those gaiters and I don't thing Harry cared much for them either.

Our little convoy set off up 'Old Arthur's' with only one set of farm buildings to pass before we arrived down the 'broo' to school. There were two boggarts to pass, for there was another one, terrible to behold it was said, which haunted the farm-buildings just round the corner past the farmhouse. During spring Harry and I were too occupied in finding birds' nests, particularly the ones made by robins. They were built into the high banks, were made of moss and were carefully disguised. We would count the eggs as they increased in number, but were careful not to frighten the 'old bird' if she were on the nest.

It was not strange that a favourite game played by boys was centred on the horse. Ours was a quadrupeds' world. Pigs, cows and horses had finer divisions such as sow, boar, heifer, bullock, colt, yearling, filly, brood mare, and more rarely stallion or 'entire'. Farmers relied upon their horses to do all the heavy work.

If tractors had appeared at all in the Fylde they were so much in the minority that it was not worth considering; and when inevitably they did come most of the older farmers resented the change. I remember talking on this subject to old Mr. Catterall, years later, after the Second World War. He was adamant that the wide, heavy tyres of the tractor and their weight would compact the land. There may have been a lot in what he said, for a few farmers never relinquished their horses and some are returning to them.

All we needed for our horsey game was a piece of bottling string. Loops were tied round the upper arms and joined loosely at the back to form the reins. The 'horse-figure' would be in command of the driver who would pull on one arm or the other to indicate the direction and give the order to walk, trot or even gallop. Round and round and in and out we trudged in our fantasy world of sowing, reaping and mowing. Sometimes the horse-figure would kick and snort if he felt frisky. When bottling-string could not be produced out of a capacious pocket the lower edge of the back of the gansy would serve as reins. The woollen garments stretched to almost limitless lengths and we would go home with the trailing edges hanging below the backs of our knees. I expected to be smacked when I got home, and I was seldom disappointed.

Hoops, or 'bowlers', also had their phases of popularity. They were made of thin strips of iron beaten into shape by the blacksmith, and were about two and a half feet in diameter. They were guided by straight pieces of metal held in the hands. Their hooks engaged in the rims of the hoops and controlled them as they rotated.

The playgrounds were communal. The one at the back with the chestnut tree and garden shed was for the infants; the front playground was for those beyond the age of seven.

The older girls would choose their own territories in

which to hop and skip; would sometimes join the boys in playing hop-scotch, with the pitch marked out in chalk.

We might come together to take part in a round-dance. This rondo had its roots way back in history, but we innocents were unaware of its origin.

As we held hands and revolved slowly round a central figure we little knew that we were re-enacting a fertility ritual or part of a ceremony associated with witchcraft.

We sang the slow, haunting melody, not without its element of pathos, over and over again. Against the hypnotic primitive repetition the principal character in the ring changed constantly, male alternating with female.

> *"The wind, the wind, the wind blows high,*
> *The rain came pattering down the sky.*
> *(a) Hil-da Hoole, she is pretty, she is the girl*
> *of the Golden City,*
> *She goes a-courting one, two, three,*
> *Tell me, tell me, who is he?*
> *(b) George Roskell says he loves her,*
> *All the boys are fighting for her,*
> *He goes a-courting one, two, three,*
> *Tell me, tell me, who is she?*

The patterns (a) and (b) followed one after the other, evenly and regularly. Only the names were altered.

The sounds of our voices dispersed over the surrounding fields, then devoid of buildings, and swept over the neighbouring churchyard less than a hundred yards away, where yesterday's children lay sleeping. The living and the dead.

The key figures of our round-dances were really Birth and Death, alternating constantly to an unwavering rhythm. We were part of the relentless drive of the life-force which pulsated through the meadow-lands and pastures in which we were enfolded.

It seems appropriate to mention here a quaint custom, unassociated with school, but like round-dances, reaching back to antiquity.

Each Easter-time hard-boiled eggs were stained in various colours. My family never went beyond the basic pattern, immersed in coffee-grounds which were always plentiful in my great-uncle's pint mug. Some families went in for more artistic creations, multi-coloured, even with names or messages superimposed. These were not for me. Girls had their offerings placed carefully in little be-ribboned baskets, some of which were carried to church on Easter Sunday. Mother Church in the Middle Ages, being unable to subdue yet another pagan rite, had with customary shrewdness assimilated it in its own ritual.

The eggs were called 'pace-eggs'. Come to think of it, we may have gone round to each others' houses, swopping eggs. If so, elaborate hues may have enriched my collection in return for drab, uninviting ones which I proffered for exchange, such exchange being met, I suspect, with some reluctance from my peers.

Come Easter Monday little groups of youngsters, myself included, trooped along to one of the Catteralls' pastures, where we rolled our eggs down an incline or gentle sloping hill. For me, Mrs. Catterall is associated with this most simple of activities, for it was she who always elected herself to supervise our expeditions.

All these elaborate preparations and comings and goings did not kindle in me the wide-eyed enthusiasm which I felt for some other pursuits. I dragged myself along with the rest and rolled my eggs down banks it is true, but my heart was not in it. Nor did I care much for eating the eggs when the shells had been broken. Whether the whites were coffee-coloured or in several tints they were equally unappetising. The communal urge to roll things down slopes, I read later, went back to at least the Bronze Age.

It would be reassuring to believe that little children are still to be seen bobbing about in fields at Easter-time, for it was an innocent enough pleasure for many, and tradition is to be encouraged.

* * * *

Mr. C.W. Cooper had replaced Mr. Youngs as headmaster when I was still in the infants' class so I only came under his instruction when I was old enough to go into the top classes. He taught in the large classroom which housed the seniors. He must have managed an age range of five years, from nine to fourteen, which was the school leaving age. He did not have large numbers to deal with, but it was hard work nevertheless.

Mr. Cooper was in command of his job and did not hesitate to enforce discipline. He was both liberal and skilful in his use of the cane and his hackles would have risen had anyone mentioned depriving him of his deterrent. As some of his older pupils became more and more opposed to being taught; as the lure of the fields and the freedom there-in became stronger and as the attraction to book-learning, never more than lukewarm disappeared al-together, how else could he keep firm control except by dominance through force.

Counselling? Mr. Cooper believed as Captain Bligh did of his midshipmen. Pupils were the lowest form of animal life until they reached an acceptable standard of maturity and experience. He did not go out of his way to seek our opinions for he knew either that we did not have any, or that they were not worth listening to. He just taught facts unadult-erated by political or religious dogma and left it at that. Few people of my age who underwent a strict disciplinarian regime have much to say against it and many would wel-come its return.

I had no great rapport with Mr. Cooper; I do not think that he cared much for me, and I never liked him. I re-spected him, for as far as I could judge he was fair. He punished the rough-hewn, the resentful and those nearing the end of their 'schooling' who were bored with it. He didn't punish me because I took care that he had no cause to do so. Let us say I was cautious but not fearful in his presence.

He was always well dressed both in public and in the classroom. In the village he had a responsible and import-ant position and he upheld it. He never sprawled across his desk when he taught. His lessons were delivered standing and there was much 'talk and chalk', much of the quick fire question-answer technique. I must have benefitted for, if examinations still count, as they did then, I was his greatest success in my year.

Many of my classmates went home to chain-harrows and horsedrawn hay-rakes; to mending fences and farm implements; to cleaning the cows' udders and milking by hand.

It was not surprising therefore that importance was given to practical work, like woodwork and gardening. As I have said I had little enthusiasm for woodwork and less ability but I was at home with sums and reading and writing. In the end Mr. Cooper despaired of my disastrous attempts at joinery and sat me down away from the class to read a book. I read a series called 'Tangle-wood Tales' several times over, thus reaching the upper limits of the school library. By the time I sat for a County Scholarship, when I was nearly eleven, I had exhausted every sheet of reading material that there was in the school.

I went to Fleetwood Grammar School to take the examinations. My mother, as usual, had made sacrifices to ensure that my Christmas was a memorable one by giving me a Meccano set, I set out to make a special effort in return.

When the news came that I had been successful my mother was filled with joy. The others in the family, though very pleased, had some doubts. Quite apart from the extra cost in sending me to grammar school, they thought that it might be placing us beyond our station.

Though I had brought prestige to the school, Mr. Cooper was not exactly fulsome in his praise. He had suggested that I may not be quite the right material for a free place in a grammar school. There must be something about the look of our family which causes people to underestimate our abilities. Possibly it is because we are reticent in telling how good we are. We have become accustomed to unfavourable predictions and have learnt to ignore them.

Artistry and Ailments

TWO or three years before I went to 'Baines' it was arranged that I should have piano lessons. My mother, finding money from nowhere as usual, managed to buy a second-hand instrument.

A tiny young lady called Miss Storey would flutter in, all hot and dishevelled from her nine-mile cycle ride across Rawcliffe Moss from Garstang where she lived. Little Miss Storey was enveloped in woollens and tweeds of more modern design and colour than those worn by Mrs. Youngs. In cold weather she reinforced herself with voluminous scarves which took some little while to uncoil. With a large bag containing impedimenta vital to her travels, pencil and rubber at the ready, she perched herself on the edge of a chair next to where I was placed at the keyboard and chirped me through a lesson. She would make appropriate marks on the music with her pencil to reinforce a point or to accentuate a difficult passage. She was gentle in her tuition and I offer her my thanks for her patient guidance.

The only fault, alas, a most common one, was in my own reluctance to practise. To my mother's credit, she made me do it, and it was thanks to her and of course to Miss Storey that I reached beyond the level to which most young players go.

My grandmother, hovering in the background, muffling the oven door when necessary, for both piano and kitchen were in the same room, always produced a refreshing cup of tea for Miss Storey to sip and a freshly baked cake or two for her to peck at, as she sat there surrounded by appetising smells. Miss Storey twittered her appreciation and my grandmother simpered, almost responding with a curtsey, for she set Miss Storey on the same level, or almost on the same level as those gentlefolk, the Misses Barlow, for whom she had worked. My grandmother spoke the Lancashire dialect with a genteel accent all of her own. When talking to such people as Miss Storey or Mrs. Gornall, the vicar's wife, she would cause me secret amusement by making special efforts at refinement.

Miss Storey, having completed her refreshment and having displayed her breeding by expressing her thanks, now enfolded herself in her protective coverings, put her large bag on the handlebars where it swung precariously, mounted her bicycle and made her way, rather insecurely, down the narrow lane to the next victim.

I was left to practise. One tune which I played was in waltz-time. It possessed none of the vitality of the Viennese waltz. Because of its depressing theme it was marked 'Lento'. The words set to this melody were so sad that my grandfather was attracted to them like a moth to an open flame. "Underneath the gas-lights' glitter", ran the first line, the only one I can remember. It went on to tell of an unfortunate girl, ragged, underfed and soaking wet, who stood on the cobblestones which glistened in the darkness. She was attempting to sell matches, but had met with no success. The dice was loaded against her; she had nothing going for her at all. There was a picture of this pathetic, underprivileged creature which, with typical Victorian obsession with adversity, squeezed compassion to the last drop. One could sense the haste with which my grandfather rushed home to identify more closely with the lonely, the unwanted, the unloved of whom he had probably been thinking all day long.

I spoilt it for him by fumbling for, or by striking incorrectly the low note in the left hand which came on the first beat of each bar, thus arresting the rhythmic continuity; or by playing a B natural instead of a B flat in the right hand melody, thus ruining completely the piercing dramatic effect. He looked at me with disapproval for having robbed him of the pleasure of his agony and took himself off with disappointment to his chair in the corner by the fire.

As well as having a fascination for ghostly topics, as I have described, my family also had an appetite for sickness and death which was above the average. Societies both civilized and primitive have rituals attendant upon the dead. As death had been such a familiar visitor for centuries up to about the time of my arrival in the world, it was not surprising that Hambleton churchyard was a favourite meeting place for many of the quick as well as the dead. To our family it seemed to have a stronger, magnetic effect.

For all members of the Church of England, active, as we were, or inactive, as were others, it went without saying that one's last journey would be to the village churchyard. It was a comfort to look up the path as one went past and to know that there, waiting, was plot of earth of one's own which had been reserved for years. All that was needed was to be dropped neatly into place alongside other members of the family, still together and awaiting the Last Judgement among a growing number of acquaintances, friends and dare one suggest, a few erstwhile enemies who had crept in.

My grandfather, my grandmother and also my mother in their periods of self-flagellation of the spirit would sigh and remark that "the sooner the better they were in Hambleton churchyard". They would be contemplating from above their earthly shells lying prostrate and peaceful beneath the friendly ground, their hard stint on this mortal coil at an end. My great-uncle, not being of such a romantic turn of mind did not dwell overmuch on the inevitable, for he was not too keen on the prospect of, as he put it, "grinning at a board" for ever and ever.

On fine afternoons small parties of ladies could be descried hurrying up Church Lane on their way to the churchyard. They would carry bunches of flowers to place on the graves of their families. Having paid their respects they would stroll round the paths and between "the serried ranks assembled", reliving the olden times, recollecting old friends and anticipating their own passing.

It was, of course, expected that I, a bonafide resident of the village and an accepted member of a well-established family, would rest there one day. Entrants from outside were not really welcomed except through marriage, which was acceptable. What would be the reaction now, if it were possible for the occupants to sit up and view new inmates and to read new names on gravestones. "What strange new faces, not Lancastrian in origin, what strange, 'outlandish' names".

In my day a 'passing bell' was tolled on the death of an inhabitant of the village. In the mysterious manner in which the 'grapevine' works, everyone knew when a person was near to death. On hearing the resonant, funereal tone of the bell, then housed in an old crenellated tower, workers in the fields within a couple of miles radius — for the sound carried on a still day — would pause for a moment or two and reflect on the person who had died.

The custom no longer survives; the bell no longer echoes from the same tower. A new structure has been erected to replace it. It stands there, an idiosyncrasy if ever there was one, product of a new environment which it overlooks with supercilious dominance.

Whatever it is or is meant to be, I venture to suggest that its presence would attract the strongest resentment and the most acerbic comments from those resting in its shadow who were old when I was young.

Tuberculosis, or consumption as it was more commonly called, was still very much to be feared. There was one family which had inter-married with either my grandfather's or my grandmother's side, which had brought consumption with it. It was more prone to visit younger folk. They were said to "go into a decline". The cure, which was by no means infallible, was absolute rest and as much fresh air as could be absorbed. Great sanatoria were built up and down the country, on sites chosen for the health-giving air about them. The patients, though isolated, could be seen lying exposed on their verandahs in all weathers.

Whooping cough, diptheria and scarlet fever were all potential killers, as were bronchitis and pneumonia. With pneumonia there was very little that could be done except to let the patient literally "sweat it out", until finally the crisis was reached, when everyone held his breath and hoped that the corner had been turned successfully. Uncle Ben tells a fearsome story of a servant-man who was struck by this disease. He was left, covered with sacking, on the landing of Clay Gap Farm, where he worked. His fever raged so fiercely that during the night he drank a lading-can full of water, upwards of a gallon, which had been left as sole companion in his ordeal. I do not know whether he survived his crisis.

Sepsis or blood-poisoning caused more than a passing concern. In a farming area where accidents, cuts and bruises were commonplace, there was the ever-present risk of infection, particularly as the injured were stoical in their suffering and were likely to be careless in keeping out the dirt. It is hard to imagine the absence of an extensive range of potent antibiotics, but then there was only recourse to ointments, salves, often of dubious value, and the lancet. A doctor would reach for his lancet and with a deft stroke (one hoped), send the pus spurting ceiling-wards. Though this gave temporary relief, there was no guarantee of a cure. Even nowadays there is always the chance that an infection cannot be suppressed and the patient dies, but in comparison such a fatality is rare.

Lesser afflictions were boils. Everyone suffered from boils at one time or another. Sometimes they attacked in packs, like U-boats, either collectively or in succession.

Scalding-hot bread poultices were the standard dressings, but for those irruptions which were stubborn, like mine, they had to be reinforced with Epsom salts or fat bacon. Fat bacon was the panacea for many ills. It had eased my croup for one thing, you remember. Ancients like my grandparents extolled the merits of cow-dung, applied hot. Yet it was never applied to me. It was probable that my grandmother, who had a marked distaste for excreta and its mention, would not permit it to come near the house.

In my very early teens, having profited from the tuition of Miss Storey, I was able to take an examination in pianoforte. As one might have predicted, an enormous boil arose on the back of my neck. It grew and grew, ripening to perfection on the very eve of the exam. My head was thrust forward so much that I adopted the stance of a vulture.

Prior to the examination a steaming bread-poultice was clamped on the throbbing, inflamed mass. The poultice had been fortified with a big dose of Epsom salts, and a piece of fat bacon was placed on top for good measure. I watched the poultice hiss and bubble as my mother prepared it and before she finally advanced on me to 'clap' it on my neck. My thin legs executed the ritual dance performed by all poultice-recipients as my feet beat a frenzied tattoo on the flags of the kitchen floor. My shrill cries rent the air to no avail. The poultice was secured in position with a large bandage.

As I climbed the steps of the building where I was to perform, I assisted the chemical changes which were going on under the bandage by stumbling up the steps in my unstable shoes to such an extent that the boil gave me a last spiteful stab as it burst. Tremendous relief was mine. I went on to give, if not a concert performance, a playing of my pieces adequate enough to satisfy the examiner.

Like the majority of people, my great-uncle suffered from boils at one time or other. It need not be stressed that he was not one for finesse. When he had eight boils simultaneously, all on one leg he put a strip of fat bacon on each. As one might have guessed they were tied on with bottling-string.

There was a very old white-washed cottage next door to Ingol Cottage. In it lived an elderly couple. The wife died of cancer, or a tumour as it was then called, very slowly, and her cries of agony could be heard by passers-by. If morphia was administered it did little or nothing to suppress the pain.

Each of us carries about with him a latent fear of sickness and death. It ebbs and flows according to circumstances. I think this fear was closer and nearer to the surface when I was a child. Hospitals were still places to which people were sent to die. Miraculously a transformation has taken place and in them one is now more likely to be re-born.

Abdominal operations were very risky indeed. Chloroform or ether were the anaesthetics mainly in use and their violent after-effects did not expedite the recovery of the patient.

During the whole of my boyhood I only entered a hospital once, when I went to visit my grandfather. From the impression implanted then, and from looking at photographs of the period, the whole atmosphere spelled austerity. The severity of the regime was present everywhere, from the lay-out of the wards to the long stiffly-starched aprons of the staff which crackled as they walked. From matron to sisters to staff there was not only rigid discipline but also subjection. The patients were at the end of the chain where they should have been at the beginning, and appeared to be at the mercy of those whose purpose was the dispensation of mercy.

The operating theatre, never the most welcoming of places, had a rigid, cold, menacing quality, whereas those of today, fitted with the latest technological devices are in contrast, reassuring.

Childish impressions aside with all the bias involved, we of the late Twentieth Century have every good reason to cry out in admiration at the beneficial advances in all aspects of medicine which are available to all. Nevertheless, with these advantages, undreamed of until recently, we are never content and like the pampered creatures we have become, constantly cry out for more.

My great-uncle was not one to be pampered. On a cold winter's evening he came in from the coalhouse where he had been working. He held out his left hand to show his sister. "Sitha, Liz", he said, looking quizzically at his hand.

My grandmother and I saw that it was swollen and discoloured and that a wedge of wood had lodged between the index finger and the one adjoining, forcing them apart. He had been chopping wood for kindling when the accident had happened.

My grandmother urged him to go to the doctor. The idea was rejected, for my great-uncle had a low opinion of the profession in general, and most particularly of the doctor who attended us, whom he looked upon with derision.

He spent a very restless night. Next morning even he was alarmed at the appearance of his hand and took himself off to the doctor's. On his return he allowed us to look in a matchbox in which reposed the splinter of plumtree. He never complained of the pain he must have suffered from the extraction. He expected to be treated as he would one of his horses, no better, no worse. He did not look upon himself as being any different from any other living thing, and went out of his way to avoid preferential treatment.

Normally, my great-uncle would have resorted to what was to him an infallible remedy. On a ledge in the coalhouse he kept a jar of Stockholm Tar, useful for dabbing on to animals' wounds. It was also very effective when applied to the bare backsides of fowls to stop 'feather picking'. In the jar there rested a battered old brush. Coal dust had settled on the greasy sides of the jar and the whole had a most insanitary appearance. He would daub a liberal amount of this glutinous substance on to a graze or cut. He had good healing flesh and apparently a formidable resistance to bacilli, and two or three days would see him cured.

From Harvest to the Academic

HAY-TIME and harvest were good times for lovers. Instead of meeting in the darkness and crouching in nooks and corners of wind-swept farm-buildings, they could enfold themselves in each other's arms amidst the 'haycocks' or 'attocks' of corn, having first selected a spot secure from prying eyes.

I was free from the distraction of courtship as I sat in the bottom of Mr. Catterall's hay-cart along with several other children, probably Hilda included and certainly Harry, as we travelled and lurched along dried up cart-tracks on our way to the hayfield.

We knew when they were carting hay. We rushed out of school to change into our playing clothes, snatching a bite to eat on our way out. With the benevolent permission of the Catterall menfolk, we would clamber up the spokes and tumble into a cart or seat ourselves on the flat floor of a lorry. We needed no telling about legs dangling over sides for we were aware of the danger of them being entrapped in wheels.

The cart was sturdy, with some ornamentation, and was made of wood. It had two great dish wheels fitted with great spokes. Each wheel was hooped with a wide iron band. For harvest times, whether for hay or for corn, a sturdy slatted projection was secured both front and back. The front one extended over the horse's hind-quarters. These extensions were called 'fleyks' and they increased very considerably the base on which the load would rest.

In normal circumstances the hay would have undergone

a process or two before it was put into 'cocks', or heaps, which varied in size according to the whims of the farmer whose hay it was. The locality also had something to do with it. In one field there were very small cocks. not even a respectable forkful in each, whilst in another the cocks were little haystacks in themselves.

The hay was flung up by hand on hayforks. The loader, an expert intent on creating a straight load, would rise higher and higher as he skilfully put each forkful in place. At the end, when no more could be put on, either in consideration for the horse, or, if the hay was 'light', for fear of shedding the load, the whole was secured in position with ropes.

Whilst all this intense work was going on we would be playing among the haycocks, jumping on or rolling over them. If we became too turbulent or we got in the way we might receive a mild rebuke. For all our healthy high spirits I think we were easy enough to say. A very special privilege would be ours when Mrs. Catterall, all enveloping in her motherliness, would include an extra basket for us, for 'drinkin' or 'baggin'. We would sit with the men as they took their short rest from loading, and join them as they ate and drank.

We accompanied the cart back to the barn or haystack. We had to walk unless it was a small load, the last incomplete one from the field, or a little load of 'rakings' when we could ride on top.

Back in the barn the cart was backed into position, the ropes were taken off and unloading began. The horse stood patiently the while, never moving except to flick off a fly or to stamp a foot. If the 'moo' or pile of new hay was still near to the ground we clambered on and ran about stumbling, or slid down to the floor, only to scramble up again. It was hot and dusty and more often than not we were covered in hay-seeds. We went to bed tired out whilst it was still light. I don't think my grandmother liked hay-time because it meant more washing for her, but I did, especially if the next day was a Saturday. Then there would be the newly-shaven field, yellowed and ready to be re-born and grow again, the verdant hedgerows, often untrimmed, in which wild roses blossomed in abundance; the white flowers of the blackberries which had lately replaced the brilliant yellow of the gorse, and which promised an abundance of fruit in the autumn.

From a shaded bank of a pond in one corner of the field, on the opposite side of which cattle made their drowsy way to drink, one could look down into the clear water in the space between the luxuriant growth of water-lilies and wait for the shoals of roach, glinting silver and red as they glided past. Every day was a fine day at hay-time, for if it wasn't we were forced under cover, in a calf shed, temporarily out of service for the summer, or barn, or at home, knelt on the sofa staring through the window, waiting disconsolately for it to come fine.

The cart on to which we were so eager to climb when the rain stopped may well have been made in its entirety by Mr. Joseph Hoole, Hilda's father. He had, like several others in the village, known what trench warfare was like. He had returned safe home, after serving with the 'King's Own' and was now working for the people who owned the 'Joiners' Shop' at Ryecroft Corner. When I started at my new school I passed Oak Cottage and the shop on my way to catch the Ribble bus. I would see him busy in the yard on most mornings. I passed the time of day and raised my cap and he never failed to reply cordially.

He very rarely paused in his work. One of the great handsome carts would be taking shape and I could watch it brought to its splendid completion. I admired his skill immensely and surprisingly enough, could have been attracted to the trade had I been allowed to help in creating such a compact vehicle.

Mr. Hoole was a wheelwright. He might be preparing to construct a great wheel when I went to school. On my return the spokes might be fitted each at a different angle to take the strain. He might even be 'sweating on' the great

Oak Cottage situated near Ryecroft Corner at start of incline once known as "Ballards' Broo".

iron band which had to fit tightly or it would soon work loose.

In the shop was ordered disarray, for though the joiners knew exactly where they could lay their hands on their own specific tools, there never seemed to be any time to remove the shavings which flew wildly from their planes and chisels. I picked my way knee deep in these shavings and stood well away from the feverish activity of the workers, taking very great care to avoid flying elbows.

Every kind of skill related to the farm and to do with wood came the way of men like Mr. Hoole. They started a job and saw it through from beginning to end, whether it was a cart or a hen-cabin. They took personal pride in their ability. They had a further reason for doing this, if indeed they needed one. They knew their output would be on show for the whole countryside to admire or to deplore.

* * * *

I became a pupil of Baines Grammar School, Poulton-le-Fylde in September, 1931, when I was eleven. The school, a good provincial grammar school, had been founded in 1717 by a benefactor called James Baines. 1717 was inscribed on the impressive badge on blazer and cap. The badge also carried the daunting and salutary motto "Nil Sine Labore" — "Nothing Without Work". We were never allowed to forget our benevolent founder. There was a Founder's Day Service each year in his honour, and prayers were said in his memory. The School Song was sung on this occasion of course, and at other times during the year, just to keep us in line. There was no modesty about its opening:-

> *"Founder, from whom we proudly trace,*
> *The glories of our Baines' race . . . "*

Later in the song, with splendid verbal imagery imitative of the motets and anthems of the seventeenth century, the music of F. Rawes, B.A., who led us at the organ, rose to almost inaccessible heights in a descant to the words:-

> *"Higher let our voices rise*
> *And swell the choral descant to the skies . . . "*

There was nothing wrong with stiff doses of loyalty, pride, nationalism and patriotism, unashamedly and regularly applied. The same clean-cut boys and youths who spoke such words of praise in the school hall were, but a few years later, to respond most generously when called upon to defend the country which they had been so brought up to love.

The school itself, when I first saw it, was anything but impressive. Apart from a small brick building which had been the original school the rest of it consisted of large, substantial wooden huts. Across the playing fields, however, there was a very fine building in the final stages of completion. This was to be the new school into which I moved in 1932.

On three or four occasions I have experienced changes which engendered disturbing doubts as to whether I was capable of meeting the challenges they presented. My first encounter of this kind was during my first weeks at Baines.

Everyone knows that when a child changes schools it is pretty certain that there will be psychological tremors of one kind or another. Mine were more disturbing in that I did not side-step from one school to another in the same district. From the sheltered security of my cottage, I was transported beyond the "perimeter fence" which was the natural boundary of the River Wyre and projected into the restless, competitive and often aggressive society which lay outside.

Myself, at ten or eleven years of age.

I was thrown into contact with a host of strangers who, because they lived in Blackpool and Fleetwood, already, by comparison, had the bearing of sophisticated men of the world. The large staff, all men, strode about purposefully in their gowns and directed us with self-confident authority.

The timetable was formidable in its content; a relentless torrent of homework came my way. When bells rang we leapt from one classroom to another for different lessons. The laboratories, with their sinks and taps, their array of glass piping and curiously shaped bottles were as strange to me as they would have been to primitive man.

Everything was new — and big. The country cousin had

come to town on a very protracted visit. He looked around with a wild surmise, cautiously, like a stray cat which had not yet made up its mind to trust its new master.

Would I have been happier had I not seen the other side of the fence; had not been entered for the academic stakes; had remained ignorant of some degree of scholarship; deprived of a lasting enjoyment which the Arts has provided? If I had worked out my life as a farm-servant as my ancestors had done; had laboured contentedly day in day out in an environment virtually devoid of leisure, lulled by the continued rotation of the seasons, myself a part of them; had been content with little and had received little in return; had ended my days as I began, with nothing to pass on to my children except possibly a certain native wisdom which they would be more than likely to reject — would I have been happier?

I suppose I could have kicked and yelled as I had done with my poor old grandmother. As it was I made no protest. I settled in, integrated with the worldly ones and unknowingly became more and more remote from my village and my contemporaries who lived there.

Down the Village lived a half-cousin of mine, Stanley Arthur Bowman. I think that he must have been a year in advance of me at Baines, for it was he who initiated me in the strange new ways to which I had to adjust. When I called for him on the way to the bus, his mother, Ada, and his father, Frank, always greeted me most cordially. Stanley's father, running his business from West Lodge, was usually in a hurry but Ada, one of nature's gentlewomen, never other than elegantly groomed even at such an early hour, always found time for a kindly or encouraging word. When I had grown up and was either following one profession or training for another, I made a point of calling to see Ada when I came home to Hambleton, to tell her how I was getting on. Her warm reception and her genuine interest never varied.

We of the 'over-Wyre' contingent worked to a very tight schedule. Having alighted from the bus, we had to hurry to arrive at school on time. Often school assembly would have begun without us. Many a time we had to creep in at the back of the hall, and in the early years, strain our necks and stand on tip-toe to see and hear what was going on up at the front.

There was one distinction which soon became obvious to my new school. Two separate species resided side by side in the same seat of learning. One was called 'fee-payer', the other, exempt from fees, was called 'scholarship boy' placed there by the good offices of the Lancashire County Council. The fee-payer may or may not have had as much academic ability as the other kind, but as he filled the treasure chest it was only natural that he would be looked upon rather more favourably than his poorer relations. I will not go so far as to say that there was actually intentional discrimination, for Mr. F.J. Stafford, M.A., M.Ed., would have discounted it, but the feeling was there. We were the Mark Linleys who co-existed with the Harry Whartons and Billy Bunters of our provincial Greyfriars.

Furthermore, fee-payers did not need to justify their existences through pressures brought to bear at school, but the scholarship boys did. We were put in the 'A' Form, and there we had to stay, striving always to sustain our position or to improve it. This was not a bad thing in itself. Just now there is a fad for discrediting competition; neither a winner nor a loser be. Everyone and no-one will be first. It will pass, for the very structure of society survives through one man striving against another.

Our own struggles were perpetual, partly through pride, partly because we knew that if we sank too far questions would be asked and we could be demoted from our positions and transferred to another school, which was considered a shameful thing to happen. I was the only scholarship boy at the time who travelled from Hambleton, but there were two or three fee-payers.

* * * *

Joseph Singleton,
alias 'Little Joe
in 1933.

Back in the old homestead I escaped from my brown blazer edged with yellow, disposed of my cap, laid aside my school-bag for attention later and hurled myself helter-skelter down the Village to find 'Little Joe'. He was younger than I and was related in some distant way, but I could never be bothered to unravel the genealogical complexities involved.

Little Joe's parents, Dick and Lizzie, lived in a white-washed cottage on the left "down the Village". The ceiling was low and beamed, the windows were small, the walls thick. The roof may still have been thatched. The cottage had stood for hundreds of years. Off the kitchen, or living-room, was another down-stairs room which was always referred to as a 'chaumer'. It was only when I read 'The Mylleres Tale' that I realised it was straight out of Chaucer, a survival of the Middle Ages, with its roots in France.

> *"Thus passeth forth al that ilke Satyrday,*
> *That Nicholas stille in his chambre lay*
> *And eet, and drank, and dede what him leste*
> *Till Soneday the sonne was gone to reste".*

The dialect which we all spoke and which I pride myself on being able to speak only survives in isolated pockets still resistant to change. Television and radio have accelerated an urge to 'speak properly' at the expense of the dialect, which is a pity. As in all languages there are some turns of expression which cannot be translated literally without losing their subtle effects. I enjoy speaking 'Lancashire', but alas, there are few left who can speak it with me. Should I, my Uncle Ben and Arthur ever unite in conversation, then I promise you "there'd be summat goo-in on", with great bursts of laughter interspersed. But we should be the ones who would appreciate it most.

Joe's mother was called 'Little Lizzie', an affectionate title well deserved, though I myself would never dream of addressing her in that way. She was small and birdlike as her husband was big and solid. With very little wheedling on our part Lizzie could be sweet-talked into frying us the most delicious chips.

Mr. and Mrs. Singleton, (Lizzie and Dick), Little Joe's parents

Little Joe and I must have consumed hundred-weights of chips doused in gallons of vinegar at Lizzie's table. I do not recall whether Joe's little sister Olive, a shy retiring child, joined us in our feasts.

Dick, who worked for the Council, like my grandfather, had been elevated to foreman or overseer. He was ambitious in that he kept poultry in the large orchard at the back of the cottage and tended a garden which ran through to Paul's Street, then a narrow cindered track which came out by the chapel near Ryecroft Corner.

Dick's poultry ranged freely in their extensive run, for the 'deep-litter' system and worse still the battery system had not yet arrived in Hambleton. The hens were fortunate in receiving the attention of a very fine cock which ran with them. There were always two or three cockerels ready to supplant the master cock when senility overtook him. The countryside of my boyhood rang with the crowing of cocks and cockerels. Now their sturdy, challenging cries are rarely heard. Their absence is brought home to me when I visit France, where these familiar sounds still reverberate and transport me back to my childhood.

There was a phase when Dick's resident cock failed to rise to expectations. Chaunteclere was not as assiduous in his duties to his "sustres and paramoures" as he might have been. The reason for this was that Little Joe and I had run him nigh unto death. I was becoming more and more an evil influence on Little Joe. How he remained my friend, how he retained any vestige of liking for me, I cannot imagine. Yet Little Joe still speaks and seems glad to see me.

The vendetta on the cock was all my doing. When Lizzie was busy rattling her dishes in the kitchen and when Dick was far away, busy with his over-seeing, we would creep stealthily into the hen-run and seek out the cock. He would see us coming and would flee terror-stricken in an effort to escape. His ploy was to weave in and out of the trees, but as there were two of us he couldn't win. Finally he had to give in through sheer exhaustion. I can see him now, leaning on one leg against the side of the hen-cabin, eyes glazed, comb dropping, and taking in great gulps of air. He is the only bird I have ever seen which has leant against anything for support.

There were repercussions, however. When Dick put down some eggs to hatch, as was his yearly custom, and when no chicks arrived, he was upset. The accusing finger was pointed at Chaunteclere for his inadequacy and infertility and he was removed from office, summarily executed and ended up in Lizzie's pot. I think Dick suspected then, or had Lizzie tipped him off? When a new cock took over a new regime was instituted and Little Joe and I were barred from the hen-run for life.

Prelude to Christmas

JUST as the approach to summertime was the time for thinking of tumblings over haycocks and for tumblings of a different kind by lusty, inarticulate swains and their nubile partners, Christmas and the weeks coming up to Christmas was another period of exciting anticipation.

The nights had closed in, running down to the shortest day. With the oil-lamp lit, a good fire to lie in front of on the rug, with reading and drawing and painting, with counting and examining my collections of cigarette cards for the hundredth time; with jig-saws and the playing of games involving dice and counters if a partner could be ensnared, there was always plenty to do. Later, there was my Meccano set and during term-time, my homework.

There was also a bird, a ringed dove of advancing years. In such an imaginative family as ours it was passing strange that this ancient fowl should have remained nameless, being always referred to as 'Th'Owd Bird'. This insignificant title was even more strange when compared to that which my grandmother's cat answered. She was called 'Tinseller'. Even the redoubtable Mrs. Youngs, who, through wide and varied experience could take most things in her stride, gave off vibrations of the utmost disbelief when she dragged it out of me, for there was no such name. Our cat, it appeared, had a name unique in the annals of feline history. I was loathe to tell people, for it caused me embarrassment.

When ennui overcame me, and I sought a respite from

76

my various activities, I would release Th'Owd Bird from its cage and endeavour to engage in friendly disport. Though amicable enough, it remained aloof to my advances with a dignity befitting its years, and hopped about under table and sofa, always evading my efforts to clutch it.

Alas! One springtime Th'Owd Bird looked up from its cage which hung on a wall out-of-doors in the daytime, saw and heard the amorous twitterings and pairings in the trees above, felt instinctive stirrings in its breast and decided upon a last fling. Casting caution to the wind it escaped, no one knew how, and ascended with some arthritic protestations from its wing-joints into the great out-yonder. Civilization must soon have taken its toll. It could not compete with the hard-nosed lot it had been so eager to meet. No-one had warned it that society does not accept newcomers readily. Th'Owd Bird failed to return from a mission which had promised so much. After extensive but fruitless searches it was assumed that Th'Owd Bird had perished; the empty cage and some photographs being the only mementos of its having ever existed. The whole family mourned Th'Owd Bird, including, I think, my great-uncle, even if he did put on his act of studied indifference.

Travelling backwards through time for over fifty years, trying to understand my grandfather's feelings, I cannot believe that in his old age he was wildly enthusiastic about Christmas, though I suspect that partly for my sake, if not wholly, he went along with my childish excitement. Once he and his brothers and my great-uncle, and indeed my grandmother, had revelled with the best, going to the houses of the gentry, carol-singing. They had become wondrous merry, or the men-folk had (for it was not proper for ladies to take more than a sip of sherry-wine), with alcoholic refreshment proffered and accepted, until voices had lost some quality of tone and diction some of its clarity. Now my grandfather seemed to want nothing more than to sit undisturbed in his corner, puffing slowly at his pipe, with here and there a sentence or two exchanged with Lizzie, his wife. He must have dreaded the disruption of his tranquility.

As for my great-uncle, well, he resented any change or intrusion whatsoever throughout the whole of the year, never mind Christmas. But the festive season was particularly bad for him, for he saw food being prepared which he not only rejected because it was way beyond his flukes - mussels - cockles - currant - cake - pickles - blackpuddings and spoon - standing - up - in - coffee menu. Whatever would my great-uncle have thought of wine-bars and flying pizzas with Yuppies flocking in droves, of chillis, ratatouille, moussaka, lasagne, Chinese take-aways and donner kebabs. It does not bear thinking about.

Invitations were exchanged at my mother's instigation, for she was the one with the advanced ideas and the yearning for socialising. People were creatures my grandfather did not want round him a lot, except his immediate family. People to my great-uncle were objectionable things, like festering sores upon his person, with one or two notable exceptions like Miss Elsie West, who did make a very favourable impression upon him and who will make her brief entrance on the stage in a later chapter.

So the weeks before Christmas then, from October onwards, were to some only a welcome relief from monotony. The first job was the Christmas cake. This was to be no factory product, scientifically controlled to the last milligramme, the last currant, hygienically sealed in plastic cover, each one an exact replica of the other. This was to be no fat-free, sugar-free, low calory edition of a cake. There were to be no holds barred and to hell with the consequences, so long as it tasted good. Ours was an individual cake. Because of certain permutations with the contents and the baking of it, it was ours, and ours alone.

With my mother home from work earlier of an evening, the big table would be cleared for action. Raisins, sultanas, currants appeared in their paper-bags as did eggs, butter — real butter from a neighbouring farm, sugar, flour and glazed fruit and cherries. Having no deep insight into culi-

nary matters, and no claim at all to sophistication, I make
no apology for omissions. There may have been other things
as well. But the crystallized orange and lemon segments,
glistening in their sugar coats appealed to me. They were
cut into tiny segments and I, not merely present to give
moral support, would taste these delicacies until, as my
grandmother said I was "enough to try the patience of a
Saint". My grandmother, secretly proud of the knowledge
she had passed on to her daughter, would be seeing to the
oven so that at the precise moment it would be ready to
receive the cake.

Into the big brown mixing bowl, itself glazed, went the
rich mixture, which was stirred until it was just the right
texture. A liberal libation of rum was added to give even
more body. This glutinous mass then went into a tin, lined
with grease-proof paper. There was I waiting, trying patience even more, to claim my perks, to run my fingers
round the bowl for the bits that were left, and to lick the
wooden spoon.

As the cake stayed in the oven, a 'slow' oven, for hours,
my mother, would do some smoothing, until the small
hours; or would resort to her crocheting, a skill in which she
excelled whilst her eyesight allowed.

Occasionally, even the best of cooks would suffer the
indignity of having a cake drop in the middle, but all our
cakes, Christmas or ordinary, seemed to turn out all right
and had gently-rounded tops.

Another test would be when the cake was cut, for if the
fruit had collected soggily towards the bottom, the mixture
had been too moist. But our cooks were too wise to fall into
that trap and there was an even distribution.

The mince-meat would come next I fancy, again our own
brand, then the pudding.

This was placed in a large basin, covered with a muslin
cloth and tied at the top. It was boiled in our biggest black
pan (not the small one used for my great-uncle's delicacies),
for from six to eight hours.

Come the week before Christmas the women-folk, especially my mother, became bewitched. Had she not have been there my grandparents and my great-uncle would hardly have known that Chrismas had come and gone, were it not for the couple of days holiday. As it was, carpets and rugs were taken out and beaten, curtains taken down and washed, for coal-fires caused dirt to accumulate, flagged floors were scrubbed and even the stone threshold of our outside gate was 'donkey-stoned'.

Special attention was paid to the black-leading of the kitchen range. Much of this happened at the week-end with my grandfather sitting there and lifting his feet now and then and my great-uncle disappearing into the coal-house muttering imprecations as he went.

For a small household, over half of it ageing, the amount of baking was to say the least extravagant, particularly as we were by no means well off. Mince-pies and confectionery with extravagant names to match the prodigality in number leapt in and out of the oven with military precision. My grandmother's oven-cloth worked overtime.

Maids of honour, fairy buns, Goosnargh cakes — what name I wonder was given to those small, delicate circular creations, reminiscent of shortbread but much less compact? They were loaded, absolutely loaded with butter and sugar and if that was not enough, a sprinkling of fine sugar was added before they cooled. Each one fell apart in the mouth. Eastern potentates, already satiated in gastronomic indulgence, would surely have greeted these comfits of my mother's with ecstasy.

How spoilt and favoured I was; how little did I know it, having no other household with which to compare. It was only later that I came to appreciate being part of such a loving, caring and competent family.

Running concurrently with domestic preparations were external activities, equally anticipatory and exciting. I have vague recollections of appearing in school plays in the Reading Room, and of trestle tables on which stood sandwiches and cakes and jellies; and of rushing about in play afterwards and of shrill childish voices; and of my grandmother's appearances in her long, pleated bonnet, come to take me home. Yet these memories are not nearly as powerful as those of parties and dramatic productions which were given at the Sunday School.

The ones to which I refer must have been when I was very young — seven, eight, nine — for they took place in the old building, before the new wooden one was added. Its internal appearance was positively Dickensian with its high ceiling and distempered walls, with no effort made to disguise the big iron stove with the pipe leading upwards to its outlet. Only on ceremonial occasions such as important meetings or concerts was this stove permitted to show its full powers, which were formidable in a restricted area, for the Rev. Gornall and his Elders were frugal with the fuel. Normal Sunday School sessions in winter were spartan gatherings with knees knocking and Collects intoned through chattering teeth. The spirit might have been to some extent willing, but the flesh was weak.

On the other hand, with the stove stocked up and allowed full rein it was a different matter. When the temperature rose dampness sprang in places from the old walls and rivulets could be observed running down. Humidity was also created. Those sitting near the stove either shed their layers of outer garments in which they had travelled, or chose to keep them on to endure the simulated conditions of a rain-forest in which tropical fauna and flora would have found themselves at home. In addition to these discomforts the hardy parents, relatives and friends had to submit to that which was about to happen up there on the open stage which ran the width of the room. Such endurance, such loyalty, is beyond the reach of us in these insulated, protected times.

Farewell to Innocence

LOOKING at them objectively, Nativity plays are much the same wherever you go. Not much can be done with the plot. Stable, inn, wise men, shepherds in the fields abiding. Just as aristocratic dilettanti were said to drop in to hear their favourite singer in classical opera in the eighteenth century then drop out again, knowing exactly the point arrived at in the libretto, so can the same procedure be observed with a Nativity play.

Our shepherds, uncomfortable in their exposure on the stage, ill-at-ease in their drapes, brows garotted in strands of bottling string, sat crouched round an electric light bulb covered in pink paper. When they spoke of a cold night on the hill-side they only spoke the truth; when they shivered it was not acting, for the power of the stove did not extend to them. No warmth was transmitted from their bogus camp-fire. The Virgin Mary was carefully chosen for her frail and wan appearance. She clutched a bundle carefully wrapped in swaddling clothes in the form of a christening shawl, yellowed with age. It was as well that the Infant Jesus was concealed from scrutiny, for He would have been found to be nothing more than a faceless package of rags.

A self-conscious Joseph, moving from one leg to the other as he expounded his immortal lines in a voice less than masculine, bore a most splendid set of moustachios, more befitting a Mexican bandit. The Inn-keeper, always the brawniest and possibly not the brightest in the cast, stared into the vapour gathering over the audience on his left and stumbled over words which he had never really mastered or understood. The faces of the Wise Men were so heavily festooned in artificial moustaches and beards that only the eyes were left bare. It was as if voices were projected through birds' nests. One of these miniature 'desperados' held what looked suspiciously like a lacquered, decorated tea-caddy, like the one on Aunt Mary's mantel-piece.

Gathered in the background was the Chorus of Angels, stooped under enormous cardboard wings. At what had been decided were suitable points the Chorus gave voice, heralded by introductions on the piano.

Now everyone knows that church pianos are not like domestic pianos or even school pianos, though there are some features common to those in pubs. Church pianos are a breed apart. From whence came those of my boyhood? All such pianos that I knew were already very old, with battered cases and the most dreadful yellow keys, with always a few of the ivory covers missing. They lived in cold, uncomfortable churches surrounded by stone and marble, or in Sunday Schools, which were equally cheerless. For six days they stood silent and on the seventh a jolt was given to their felt pads by the sudden change in temperature and by the brief assaults upon them. No wonder that when the pianist made an insecure entry on the introductory bars of 'Hark! the Herald', there was a curious jangling sound. Such pianos were never in tune, never stayed in tune. Round, rich tones were quite beyond them. Furthermore, it is no secret that Sunday School pianists train at a special school where they are taught to drag one hand after the other, so that there is always an echo-effect.

The strained look of the Chorus became even more pronounced as they struggled mentally to hit the correct note. Had the singers all possessed perfect pitch, the effect would still have been unfortunate. As it was the result, when it came, was near to 'organum', a bleak and austere device sung by monks in mediaeval times. The first rows of the audience seemed to lean forward, partly to appreciate the admixture of sonority, mainly because the backless forms on which they sat did not permit any other posture.

At the final curtain there was enthusiastic applause. And why not? Had not a great deal of joy been given to little children, both during rehearsals and during the performance itself, in spite of the tense appearance of the cast. We had received lessons in learning to live and work together, in punctuality and in loyalty; we had known the overwhelming excitement of preparation and presentation at an age when it is at its strongest. Altogether it had been a very successful project. Were not the Misses Gregson, Miss Baron and Miss Gornall, the vicar's daughter, all deserving of great praise for their generous voluntary, commitment?

A homespun production can often do more for me than a modern, professional one, honed and polished to sleek perfection. In the same way I would find the forthright honesty of my great-uncle, with his natural body-oils jealously preserved, his nasal irruptions intact, his whiskers untrimmed, more honest and socially appealing than a 'megastar' image, shallow throughout, rubbed all over in fragrant unguents and painted with dyes of various colours.

It fell to my good fortune, years and years after I first trod the boards, that I became heavily involved in the production of 'musicals' in schools. Now, many more years on I still receive nostalgic letters from those who were adolescent boys and girls, telling of good influences and of enrichment transmitted to their own young families because of these activities.

Though I cannot recall my own contribution to the Nativity plays, I was in there somewhere. I do, however, remember vividly the time I played Bob Cratchit in 'Christmas Carol', if only for the physical discomfort I underwent.

It was with the greatest reluctance on my family's part, and with the greatest persuasion on mine that I was allowed to take part; for the previous Christmas I had been laid low with a cold of giant proportions accompanied by a rattling chest which defied description. In an effort to avoid a repetition, an extra insulation of Thermogene had been superimposed on my normal winter layer, covering me from bottom of rib-cage to neck. My long, thin legs supported my over-sized feet; my thin face and fair complextion were just right for the under-fed character which I was portraying. My upper body, however, in contrast was characteristically Pickwickian. As I went through my act, with artificial torso bulging and chest thrust forward like a pouter pigeon, I began to perspire. If I were seen to fidget over much with my cravat, uncomfortable in itself, it was not consciously to accentuate the neuroticism of Mr. Cratchit but to thrust back out of sight large fragments of Thermogene which were forever 'riding up' and threatening to suffocate me.

The outcome was all too predictable. So much had my pores been opened, so bathed in perspiration was I when I took my bow, that I caught an even bigger cold if that were possible, and was incapacitated for even longer.

Christmas Eve from a young child's viewpoint has not changed. He will feel it coming upon him for weeks in advance, but the momentum will increase until, on the day before Christmas he will be well nigh impossible to live with. Parents will still recoil at the additional expense. The choice is far greater and the cost relatively dearer. Nowadays Christmas starts at midsummer at the latest and is the greatest commercial venture of the year. Come Christmas Day the melancholia which descends after Christmas dinner is made even greater by the thoughts of credit cards which have been extended beyond the limits, and by the obligatory jet-setting holiday in search of the sun a l'Espana already booked but still to pay for.

My own mother's resources must have been stretched when I consider the treasures which I found in my pillowcase early on Christmas morning. My grandfather, still in on the act, playing his part to perfection, made much of the coming of Father Christmas (he rejected the term Santa Claus absolutely), and speculated on the entry via the chimney. We left a mince-pie on the hearth before we went upstairs, I in my sleeping-suit and carrying a guttering candle, to hang my stocking at the bed-foot. The stocking was ritualistic, only for bits. The pillowcase was the real receptacle.

WHEN EVERY DAY WAS SUMMER

There is no need to labour the getting off to sleep, and the awakening in the early morning to find that Father Christmas had been. A little red miniature of the benevolent visitor was sticking out of my stocking, or a little parcel. I would clamber out of bed and go to my grandfather's bedside and tug at his shirt-sleeve as he lay sleeping to tell him "He's been". Kind old man that my grandfather was, there was never a rebuff, always a reciprocal expression of pleasure.

A box of paints, jig-saws, a train set with a circular track with which my Uncle Ben played after the manner of uncles until he almost wore it out before I had a chance, all these came my way. One Christmas there was a pheasant made of metal. It worked by clockwork and strutted almost realistically when it was wound up. I never saw or have seen another one like it. The pièce de resistance was my Meccano set of Christmas 1930. By this time my 'age of innocence' was receding fast. Father Christmas was no longer a reality; Christmas had lost its magic never to return. It was I who now had to put on the act for my grandfather.

The Meccano set I knew I owed to my mother, with some contribution from the rest of the family and in subsequent years it was to give immeasurable pleasure.

What was the main dish for our Christmas dinner? Was it chicken, a turkey, a duck, a piece of pork or beef? It would not be a goose as advertised in 'Christmas Carol', for my grandmother thought it was too greasy to eat, even though we did use goose-grease as an extra measure to treat stubborn tight chests. I myself was not much interested in meat dishes, being more concerned with trifles and jellies and assorted, rich cakes and a good slice of Lancashire cheese, well matured as it always was, straight out of its muslin cover.

On Christmas night in later years, from about the time of the Meccano set, Arthur (soon to appear) and his parents would come for tea, and a plate of cold meats with well-seasoned pickles for a bite of supper. Whilst the adults sat and talked after the meal, and whilst my grandfather and Tom,

Arthur's father, took a glass or two of whisky or rum, Arthur and I would play on the floor, disturbing the peace as usual and always keeping sharp ears open for everything that was being said, so that we could discuss it and make fun of it when we were on our own.

Another night, my mother and I would go over to Land Hill for a return visit. I remember walking back through the frost-laden countryside bathed in moonlight. Such nights, like the one described by Pepys as "a most fine bright moonshine night with a great frost"; such breathless spell-bound nights with trees and hedges and even the road surfaces throwing off a myriad of tiny fairy-lights, were common to my childhood. Where have they gone? Can it be that the seasons really are changing; or does age diminish appreciation and enjoyment so much; or has overwhelming urban sophistication blurred the pleasure in simple scenes of nature?

> "Ah, bitter chill it was!
> The owl, for all his feathers, was a-cold;
> The hare limp'd trembling through the frozen grass,
> And silent was the flock in woolly fold".

The lanes were still, with never another traveller, save possibly one or two determined revellers making their way from 'The Shovels' or 'Wardleys', their cycle lamps wavering this way and that as they strove to keep on a steady course. Even the boggarts took a break on these days of Christmas. They were good times, those Christmases when all things were harmless, when the good was accentuated and the evil carefully concealed, when everyone was a friend.

Of Sport, Bomb Making, Tommy and Little Joe

A S I grew older my travels within the village extended and even went beyond into other districts. I got a bicycle on which I rode to and from school in good weather. I formed a few friendships at school and a few at home. These two relationships, the rustic and the scholastic, were kept separate. My school-friends usually came over for the day, or I went to their houses.

One of these was a C.D. Ashton who lived at Thornton. We exchanged visits, went on cycle rides, and for a special treat, rowed about in the boating-lake at Fleetwood. After disappearing for half a century he has re-appeared as a grandfather, living on the outskirts of Preston. Another gentle comrade of my noon-tide perambulations was Ben Wilmot. He reminds me that I called him Wilbur, whilst I went by the name of Elmer. Influences of the Silver Screen and the Wild West are obvious. In a decade or two, when we have shed this mortal mantle, someone out walking his dog on the edge of dusk may be startled to meet our spirits, still ambling along, still talking animatedly, wraiths of a bye-gone age. Wilbur, in recognition of previous good deeds for humanity, will radiate a pure white light; whilst I, Elmer, with my two little horns and forked tail, will glow like a red-hot coal.

But stay. Speaking of forked tails, there was at this time in the school a pupil who, for the sake of anonymity must be referred to as 'X', who could be said to possess a demoniac quality in that he had a penchant for destruction, even if it was on a small scale. This young fellow was a living paradox. On the one hand he was artistically gifted, on the other he veered towards the gruesome and macabre manifested in brief outbursts of localised violence. In short, he made bombs.

This potential terrorist had an accomplice 'Y', who, though possible so naive then that he did not realise the nature of his involvement, was an accessory nevertheless. He it was who supplied X with some of the raw material. The relationship of these two was somewhat akin to that between Little Joe and me. Compared to the skills of X, however, our experiment with calcium carbide shrunk into pallid mediocrity.

Y, pedalling to and from school on his B.S.A. Roadster, with 3 speed gears, price £4 19s. 6d. (£4.98p), presented to the casual observer only a harmless, uniformed schoolboy as he battled against the wind on his way to school, and still against it on the way home, for the wind is known for its malicious humour on the Fylde Coast. Yet had he been stopped and searched on his outward journey, his saddlebag, satchel even, might have been found to contain lengths of brass condenser piping, off-cuts from the place where his father worked.

X, waiting, relieved him of these and in due course repaired to his improvised workshop or laboratory, where he proceeded to stuff and pack the tubes with his own preparation of potassium chlorate and sugar, and to unravel Catherine wheels which he cut into lengths for the fuses.

Somewhere in the drowsy Fylde in the early 1930s there laboured this lone, juvenile armaments technician, surely ever in danger of "hoisting himself with his own petard", with the real possibility of projecting an unsuspecting passer-by or two into eternity at the same time.

The devices completed, they were ready for trials in the field. There must have been great cunning and subterfuge applied, for one such contraption at least was smuggled into Baines, where, under the eyes of masters and prefects (still busy preening and pontificating, oblivious to reality), it was set in a hedge in the school grounds. To use Y's own words, rather proudly, I thought with no evidence of remorse, "blew a bush straight out of the ground". On another expedition when X was operating on his own, a rock was dislodged from the cliffs at Blackpool; and on a further occasion X expressed great glee in recounting that a paint-bomb he had exploded in a street had sprayed surrounding property if not people. With all our indoctrination, individualism still prospered.

One wonder what happened to X. Did he find an outlet for his perverse talent during the war years soon to come? Did he go on to become an explosives expert in some mercenary army and gain posthumous fame? Or did he sublimate his destructive urge early on and settle down to manage a bank or become a solicitor?

In our village most of the boys about my age were obsessed with football. There was always a farmer who was willing to spare a bit of pasture-land to play on. The thud of the ball and the cries of the players could be heard from some distance on summer evenings. The Rev. Gornall, who had played at university and who was an enthusiast, turned up to advise and encourage.

I was not of their number. My companions were the solitary ones, the roamers, who chose a nomadic life loping about the open countryside, or beach-combing on the banks of the River Wyre.

On the playing fields of Baines I spent lonely hours, standing stationary in great puddles of water on the football pitch, clad in my hateful brown jersey with its V shaped yellow stripes, doing my best to evade the ball whilst at the same time feigning effort and enthusiasm. They saw through me though and I could not be regarded as other than a renegade. Furthermore, there was worse. I took not the slightest interest in cricket either. It was with raised eye-brows that I learnt later that one of my school-day cronies had all the while been indulging in this upper crust sport.

During our mid-day break when others were at the nets or were collected round the goalmouth practising 'shootin-in' with a singleness of purpose beyond all understanding, I would be strolling round the edges of the playing fields with Billington, talking idly of this and that. Billington, whose nickname was 'The Pelican' because of a facial resemblance to that bird, was a loner who also had a great disdain for team sports. He also was looked on with suspicion by those dashing, blue eyed, fair-haired types who were our games masters.

I think it is true to say that whilst Billington never took any exercise of any kind, I did attract a little grudging recognition when I swam in school teams against other schools. I also formed a liking for cross-country running and for throwing the javelin, so I was not entirely beyond the pale after all. Old boys will be familiar enough with the cross-country course, with T-wood as its boundary. Inter-house competition was keen (I was in Founders) and pressure was brought to bear on the reluctant and physically ill-equipped to enter for the race. Whoever stood a remote chance of gaining a point for his House ran, supervised at the starting-point by the ubiquitous prefects. It was no great burden for me, except that it was time-consuming, for I covered mile after mile of rough country on the other side of the river in my wild, headlong, unsupervised sorties. Dogged persistence was obviously a predominant quality, successfully nurtured in this "our Baines race". One at least of our number deserved the supreme accolade. He gained the distinction of being the only B.G.S. boy to come last in the 'cross country' two years in succession, subsequently gaining an announcement to that effect in 'The Poultonian'.

Swimming and bathing, especially in salt water, attracted me very strongly. As far as I know, I was the only adolescent in the village who could swim at all, and although the tidal river was five minutes walk away I was the only one who took advantage of it.

WHEN EVERY DAY WAS SUMMER

I should have worked harder at school. I could have worked harder. For my mother's sake, not for my own, I am sorry that I was so selfish. Were I able to turn back the clock, however, I doubt whether I should have the will-power or the inclination to do much better a second time.

My greatest drawback to academic achievements lay in my hedonism. Fundamentally pleasure-seeking, pleasure-loving before all else, I could not resist the charms of my 'beloved', which was the countryside in the Fylde. Her space, beauty and above all, her solitude coaxed, beckoned or dragged me away from my books.

My mother did not have the experience nor the time to keep track of my laxity; nor did my schoolmasters bother overmuch, so long as I continued to produce work of a satisfactory standard. There were no careers masters; I was never told of the possibility of gaining scholarships in higher education. No-one encouraged me to try for one. As far as I knew, those senior pupils who went on to university were supported by affluent parents who were able to pay. I never reached my 'ceiling' academically, never really knew whether it was high or low. There were still undertones of 'Edwardian Summers' in my grammar school. The teaching, though excellent in certain areas was more relaxed than it became later. The pressures applied were incomparable to ones I met when I became a teacher myself in a well-known grammar school in Leeds in the late 1950s.

I paid for my own weakness and had a lot of catching up to do in the future. Happily my mother was still alive when I repaid at least some of the obligations I owed her. For myself, I would not surrender one golden moment of my springtime. So unproductive, so wanton in its wastefulness it was to be the only time that I ever roamed free.

There were not many boys who chose to wander and explore the fields and the hedgerows, the woods and the banks of the river. Our little party of three or four at the most was familiar enough to farmers who did not object to our wandering off the public footpaths. We were not out to destroy. If we dragged ourselves along a dried-up ditch through the matted brambles no harm was done, except to our clothing. If we felt our way along the steep, soggy banks of a ditch in winter, hanging on to the stumps of hawthorn for support, nothing suffered except our stockings and boots. We saw frogs' spawn, not in jam jars but where it had been layed in ditches and ponds in which slimy green water plants grew.

Tommy (a close companion during a certain stage), and I knew all the fish-bearing ponds for miles around; knew where large roach would be feeding under the over-hanging trees on still evenings, with the midges flitting about in swarms above the deep water. We gained seemingly unattainable vantage points out along slippery boughs which extended over the ponds, cautiously dragging our rods with us. In our early days our equipment was primitive but we progressed eventually to jointed rods and reels. We were experts on the size of hook suitable for a certain species and connoisseurs when it came to choice of bait.

Usually Tommy and I fished alone, two silent figures, sometimes choosing the same spot, sometimes isolated in different stations round the pond. We might take a bucket with us to bring back the catch, for in the garden I had an old tin-bath which was my lily-pond. We might add more fish to the collection in Mr. Catterall's watering trough; or we might throw back our catch at the end of a session.

One never-to-be-forgotten incident happened on Lewtas' Hill, at a pond at the top of the long field to the left of the footpath. For some reason, Tommy's sister and one or two of her friends had forced their company upon us, which was unusual, for Tommy and I did not welcome intruders. Having cautioned the girls to keep quiet we set our floats at the correct depth after some consultation, baited our hooks and cast our lines. Silence did not reign for long. Soon my float bobbed up and down a couple of times before it ran away and was drawn under. Tommy's sister, standing close behind me could not contain her excitement. She shouted "Ed's a bite, Ed's a bite", and pushed against me accidentally. I was precipitated headlong into the pond.

The pond was by no means the purest one in our circuit. I stirred up a lot of muddy water as I spluttered about retrieving my rod and tacke, before I reached for the side and dragged myself out, wet through from head to foot and festooned with weeds. I was in a quandary of the first magnitude. How was I to explain away my saturated state at home, where my every watchful grandmother awaited me?

As our little tribe retraced its steps through the fields, I was its most miserable and reluctant member, squelching and dripping at every step. Turning left at the bottom of Market Street, my heart missed a beat for the second time that evening, for who should I spy but a very familiar figure. There was only one bonnet like that and I knew it well. It being the edge of dusk my grandmother had come to search for me.

A kind of ballet was enacted that night in Market Street. It was so unique that it captivated my little companions and drew folks away from their chairs by the fireside to gaze upon it in wonder. Sensing my grandmother's mood and wishing only to escape from it, I made a feint to the left. With a speed one would have thought quite beyond her years and hampered by her voluminous garments, my grandmother nevertheless forestalled me and I had to take immediate evasive action. Bobbing this way and that we pirouetted and weaved up the hill until I broke away, headed for home and took cover under the kitchen table, much to the consternation of my grandfather, who was sitting placidly in his rocking chair, smoking his pipe.

My grandmother was not far behind. She treated me like the half-drowned rat that I was, proceeding to poke me out with the handle of her broom. She did not heed how hard she probed or where she struck. Either she or my mother, I forget which, probably both, lashed me about my head with my own wet stockings. I was forced to take a bath in the big galvanised tub before being sent to bed in utter disgrace. It was some days before I was seen with Tommy again in our old haunts.

To return to Little Joe. We decided to conduct an experiment to investigate the explosive properties of calcium carbide. This chemical, a white rocky substance which gave off a pungent smell, was used to provide the flare for cycle lamps. A container which formed the lower part of the lamp and which screwed on was half filled with carbide and water added. A chemical reaction took place and gas was given off. The flame could be controlled by a valve. When the valve was turned on the cyclist was always accompanied by a faint hissing sound. I remember that when I was much older I was caught out one black night, way out by Cartford Bridge when my lamp ran short of water. Having heard that a good substitute was urine, I urinated in my lamp. Never had I been guided by such a bright and powerful beam; never had my nostrils been assailed by such an offensive and penetrating stench.

I suppose that I instigated the experiment with Little Joe as an extension to my researches in the chemistry laboratory at Baines. I was the chemist and Little Joe was my assistant. I led and Little Joe followed. He was quite accustomed to playing a secondary role.

The site chosen was near to that very pond where the mishap had befallen me. It was an isolated spot as befitted the secret investigations upon which we were engaged. Our equipment was not impressive. It consisted of nothing more than a large Tate and Lyle's syrup tin (Little Joe ate a lot of syrup butties) which Lizzie had discarded. A tiny hole had been pierced in the centre of the bottom. Calcium carbide was placed in the tin, water was put in and the lid was tamped down very firmly. The tin was turned upside down and positioned on the grass.

After a suitable time had elapsed for the gas to be produced, I intimated to Little Joe that he should light the touch-hole. He struck his match and gingerly applied the flame. Nothing happened. I urged a second attempt, suggesting that this time he might be a little bolder in his application. Little Joe bent right over to put the match to the hole. There was a loud explosion and a sharp, metallic crack. My calculations had proved correct. It had worked. Little Joe was flung flat on his back, clapping his hand to his forehead. When he took it away there had appeared, stamped on his forehead and the upper part of his face, an imprint of the rim of a Tate and Lyle's syrup tin. The lid remained on the ground where it had rested, but of the tin no trace was ever found.

There are three other noteworthy episodes in which Little Joe played a major role.

In the first the backcloth was the River, for we nomads were capricious creatures who demanded a constant change of scenery. We had lit a fire of driftwood, with difficulty, for the driftwood was often damp. (That is why, after a few hours spent at our encampments our eyes were red-rimmed with smoke. As we trailed our bodies homewards up the Village we smelt like itinerant bonfires). We were roasting a few potatoes which we happened to have with us. Little Joe was rooting about round some trees at the top of a steep bank, looking for some drier wood. Suddenly a voice cried out in some agitation "Dick's bin stanged — Dick's bin stanged". The voice belonged to Mr. Hull or 'Cock Hull' as he was called locally. Mr. Hull had been out shooting rabbits when he had recognised Little Joe and assessed his dilemma, even though he was a generation out with the name. Tommy and I, sitting on large stones by the fire, sprang up to see Little Joe hurtling down the bank with jerky movements as if he were a marionette.

On his face and clothing rested bees. Bees flew all about him. 'Dick' had indeed been 'stanged', attracting to himself a whole nest of bees which he had accidentally stirred into anger. We took 'Dick' home. In two or three days the pain and swelling had gone. For once I was freed from all blame, or nearly all.

One Boxing Day we dug a cave in a very steep vertical bank near to Shard Bridge. It was raw and damp and we spent the afternoon in a sitting position hacking at the wet clay. When the short day was nearly over and it was time to be heading for home, our cave collapsed. It was not a serious fall, but by the time we had slipped and slithered down the bank we were saturated and coated with clay. All of us suffered from sharp tongues and received a few blows from our guardians, the womenfolk.

With Little Joe it went further. The doctor was called in and he was put to bed for at least a week. From the bits of gossip I picked up about his condition I understood that he had a kidney infection. In those days I wasn't really interested and had little if any knowledge of where those organs were situated or what purpose they served. It was soon common knowledge that Aunt Isabel, christened Isabella, who lived a few doors away in the Village and was my grandfather's sister and Little Joe's grandmother, had been shrill in her incriminations. "That Edwin", she had cried "has nearly 'sided' our little Joe", which was just another way of saying that I had nearly killed him.

The third incident gave a further jolt to Little Joe's fickle kidneys. At one period of my youthful development, it was my custom to swim in the River even on the coolest days. Only on one occasion was Little Joe induced to follow my example. It was in a snowstorm. We both stripped off. I immersed myself immediately and started swimming, knowing from experience that after the savage initial shock I should begin to glow and tingle all over. Not so with Little Joe, who could not swim and had to be satisfied with sticking to the shallows. I swam about like a protective destroyer whilst Little Joe half-submerged himself, his white body naked and shivering.

I still felt guilty when I think of the sight of Little Joe trying to pull on his long woollen vest with the buttons at the neck and the long sleeves. It did not slip on easily because he had not dried himself properly. He shook uncontrollably, his teeth chattered and his body had turned Wedgwood Blue. As the snowflakes gathered on his vest I could not help noticing that it was inordinately long, and fell to his knees.

I ran Little Joe up and down the sand in an effort to start up his circulatory system. I was disappointed in him for his marked lack of enthusiasm, for all he could talk of was about going home.

Messages of the strongest censure were passed from Lizzie and Dick to my family. Never again did I take Little Joe with me to bathe, not even on the hottest of days.

Black Puddings and Miss Elsie West

ON re-reading Siegfried Sassoon's trilogy 'The Complete Memoirs of George Sherston', I am bound to be aware of the wide difference in the social status of George Sherston and me. He had a nursery fire to sit by; mine was communal. He had private means, I had none. He was attended by servants and from an early age had his own pony or horse. Being on the fringe of fox-hunting country he rode to hounds when he was old enough, and was socially acceptable as one of the gentry. There was no need for him to study for a profession or to engage in a business. Indeed, he displayed no inclination or enthusiasm in either of these directions.

My family, as I have intimated, were servant-orientated. They were the ones working in the stables or gardens or below-stairs. It was they who stood aside and curtseyed as the master or mistress swept past; they who held the horses' heads and deferentially touched the peaks of their caps. As I grew up, I found it more and more difficult to accept or adopt a servile attitude. Whether consciously or unconsciously, I did my best not to put myself in situations where I needed to grovel or to lick boots in order to survive. My family no doubt found it hard to understand and to condone this lack of compliance.

Being destined to be the groom rather than the rider, the pony was not for me. I should never become bow-legged prematurely through straddling the barrel belly of my pony; never parade my well-cut riding breeches; never wear a little hard black hat; never draw attention to myself in shrill tones and affected upper-crust accent. Had I, by some quirk of fortune, found myself on my little mount competing with other children at the 'Horse of the Year Show' or its 1920s equivalent, I should have needed muzzling to prevent being ostracized, penalised or ridiculed for my powerful Lancashire accent. I was stuck with it, never to lose it — not that I ever tried very hard.

My pony was my bicycle or my feet. For longer journeys there was the red-painted Ribble bus which made a round trip between Blackpool and Knott-End a few times each day. There were no foxes to hunt, no hounds. The only furry, four-legged creatures that I came near to hunting was the farmyard rat. Although I did not go out of my way to force an encounter with that rodent as I had heard of its ferocity when cornered.

Nannies and nurseries, ponies and preparatory schools only existed in story-books as far as I was concerned. I was the rough-haired one, nose pressed to nursery window, looking in on the smooth-haired at play with their rocking-horses, or eating their crumpets round the nursery fire. As far as I recall, I was curious but not at all over-awed or envious at what I saw, I was more than content with my home, the home of a working-class family, jealously guarding the raising of its own and fiercely independent in doing so. It would have broken me to have been sent away, supposedly unwanted, before I was ready.

There are always at least two ways of looking at a thing. I was later to work out that sometimes it was an act of mercy to send youngsters away from parents who were so busy with their own lives and careers that they were barely aware of the children's existence; or because their own sordid life-style did nothing to promote love and security.

It is a sad situation to have only the choice of two evils.

My great-uncle would not have adapted readily to a nanny; nor would he have taken kindly to thin slices of bread and butter at the nursery table, or to cucumber sandwiches on the lawn for that matter.

Coffee, ground for him in a coffee-mill, was put into his

pint mug and boiling water was poured over it. If he took milk it would only be a drop or two, for it was not a product which he raved about. The beverage was so strong that when he had drunk it the coffee-grounds filled half his mug. He would not tolerate a weaker brew. He had a liking for pickled onions, but they had to be at least a year old, preferably more. After two or three years they would be so matured in vinegar that they had turned black, and that is how he liked them. He would wait until my grandmother was busy with the oven, when he knew that nothing would distract her. Then he would leer across at me and wink, as he speared a vintage pickle with his thumb nail which he used as others would a fork. The nail was a horny append-age, encouraged to grow long, after the fashion affected by Siamese dancing girls. There the similarity ended.

To digress for a moment, people like my great-uncle, and there were quite a few still about when I was a lad, very seldom ailed anything. They were like ducks, either healthy or dead. Everyday ills like colds or stomach upsets passed them by, unless they happened to pick up a paricu-larly virulent germ, when they only showed mild symp-toms. Large flies which had been crawling about on middens nearby, crawled about unmolested on their food. The reluctant bacteria entered their bodies, only to be battered to death by systems which had built up a formi-dable immunity. Fat bacon which had 'gone off', or as they would say had 'gone reesty' was consumed by them with only mild intestinal disturbances hardly worth recording.

Of course, constitutions varied. Some were more robust than others, some infections more powerful. Short bouts of diarrhoea were accepted and occurred more frequently. Even the most hardy was smitten with sledge-hammer force occasionally. Uncle Ben has left a revelation of one of his work-mates on 'the thresher', an agricultural machine to which he became attached and about which there is further mention in a later chapter.

The select band of "brethren of the thresher", a jealously guarded, tiny insular close-knit community of unusual garb, appearance and manner of speech, did not always sit down to eat in an environment of fastidious cleanliness. A 'bug' of a most rare potency must have bombarded the bowels of one of my uncle's colleagues (whose first name was Jemmy), during a hasty lunch-time, so fiercely and with such persistence that after two or three days of constant urgent calls of nature, when he had to throw himself off his clamorous machine and squat behind the nearest cover at a moment's notice, he was forced to visit his doctor, most probably for the first time in his life. As my Uncle Ben said, using typical understatement, "He must a bin badly", to have resorted to such a desperate measure.

After the long day was ended, through which Jemmy had worked in spite of his increasingly debilitated condition, he set off on his bicycle along the country lanes, somewhat unsteadily one imagines, to seek professional advice. The doctor, after hearing his brief story, asked him when it was that he had last had a motion. The question had to be rephrased more bluntly in a term which he understood.

Familiar as he was with outbursts of truth stripped of refinement, the doctor must have been taken aback at the patient's reply. Out it came, quick and concise, with no attempt at concealment: "Twice on't road and once at back o' thy gate". The response of Jemmy was both normal and authentic.

The mental stability of such folk as Jemmy and my great uncle matched the physical. They lived one day at a time, not anxiously peering into the future. They had no sales target to achieve, no status to improve and to maintain. They were not introspective, not pre-occupied with self-analysis and quite indifferent to the impressions of other people. The next day was going to be the same anyway — and the next, give and take a change in the weather which was beyond their control. When they went to bed, in my great-uncle's case with a night-cap or two of stong ale, they slept undisturbed for there was nothing to disturb them.

Again my Uncle Ben tells of meeting and old farmer of this hardy school as he was going over Rawcliffe Moss. This old man told my uncle that he "wasn't so weel" as his leg was troubling him and he had "a job to keep gooin". The stiff upper-lip in some instances was not a property possessed only by the upper classes; not merely a quality confined to the playing fields of Eton. These country-folk could teach the privileged a thing or two when it came to under-state-ment. To admit that one "wasn't weel" meant that one was feeling pretty bad. To say that one was "not so bad" implied radiant health.

With great difficulty the one who had confessed that he wasn't so weel rolled up his trouser leg to reveal a great gash in the lower part of his limb. It was swollen out of all proportion and there was a tell-tale red line running up his leg. He revealed that he had a painful lump in his groin. My uncle thought it was blood-poisoning and strongly advised a doctor. My uncle's acquaintance stated categorically that he "thowt nowt o' doctors" and that he was treating himself. He took out a large bottle and helped himself to a great swallow of whisky. In what was presumably his fevered state this should have put paid to him.

My uncle watched him go on his way, for what he thought was the last time. It wasn't though. A week or two later the erstwhile sufferer was fully recovered, hale and hearty, whisky bottle at the ready. Such an obstinate atti-tude and such irresponsible treatment are not to be advised or condoned, but they worked for him.

Black-puddings were much favoured by my great-uncle. He would make trips to Poulton on foot in order to purchase these delicacies from a very good pork-butcher's in The Square. He eschewed all forms of mechanised transport. For him buses did not exist. I see him now, just returned from his six or seven mile road trip, his sack soaked through and fastened round his neck with a nail, the uneven brim of his monstrously battered old hat dripping water on to the kitchen floor, the stubble on his lived-in face studded with raindrops which glistened under the paraffin lamp which was suspended from the ceiling.

From somewhere among his layers of garments he produces a saturated bundle of newspaper in which lie his black-puddings. He offers them to 'Liz', who, without much coaxing on his part, for they have an understanding, these two, gets out a black iron pan and sets about boiling the unlovely black spheres for his supper. They are very fine black-puddings and give off a savoury odour, but I am repelled by the great lumps of white fat which are part of their structure. My great-uncle is not above giving them the attention of his thumb nail if he can get away with it, for he often dines on his own at odd hours.

Whilst the black pot is boiling I hover in the background fairly certain that there is more to come. Rarely am I disappointed. My great-uncle might delay a little, no doubt noticing my subdued excitement, but eventually he extracts another bundle which is my 'Comic Cuts'. It has to be straightened out and laid on top of the oven to dry before I can read it. The point is, he seldom disappoints me. Nor does he forget my sweets.

There is a footnote to add; an eyebrow raising revelation which was almost lost forever. Only at the time of writing has my Uncle Ben, now in his eightieth year, decided to open Pandora's box and divulge a rustic frolic which ended in tragedy. I certainly did not gain the salacious information in the 'black pudding/Comic Cuts' period. There was a conspiracy of silence on the unmentionable in our house.

That my great-uncle had chosen to remain a bachelor meant that he had chosen a life of celibacy. Bachelorhood and celibacy, as far as I was concerned at that time, were synonymous. I saw my great-uncle as a large well-mauled teddy bear, with food stains down his front which required sponging from time to time. It was indisputable that he was of the male gender, but as far as my concept of him went, the male appendages were erased. Had he known my assessment he would not have been flattered.

Referring once more to the photo of my great-uncle in his working clothes round about 1930 when he was in is seventies, it stretches credibility somewhat to discover that a presentable young women had succumbed to his amorous advances not all that long before. The old dog. Who would have believed it? When my Uncle Ben told me I sent silent congratulations to my great-uncle which stretched beyond the grave.

That he was a dapper and virile young man is beyond dispute, but the sexual encounter, as far as I can assess, took place about the outbreak of the Great War, possibly a little later. My great-uncle would have been in his midfifties but his partner was much, much younger. The lady in question, hitherto unknown but recognised immediately by my Uncle Ben, was none other than Miss Elsie West.

My great-uncle it may be remembered,

My Mother with Elsie West (seated) in what appears to be a Studio Portrait, about 1913.

had paid the rent at Model Cottage. My mother, having formed a friendship with Miss West, brought her home to tea from time to time, as was the custom. My great-uncle had obviously not missed the opportunity to assess the attractions which Miss West offered as she sat primly at table, decorously effulgent in praise of my grandmother's pastries. His observation would be from some vantage point well away from the table, for my great-uncle never

105

joined the family for a meal when 'company' was present. One can only imagine sly glances exchanged, signals passed. Beneath Miss West's embroidered bodice her heart fluttered. My great-uncle felt the fever stirring in his loins, unsuspected by all in the innocent gathering save probably Miss West.

Several assignments must have been arranged, with dalliance more than implied, judging by the result. The number of their meetings is unrecorded, their choice of meeting place for the consummation of their passion lost forever, long receded into history.

When it was found that a child was on the way my great-uncle, to give him credit, did not try to avoid his reponsibilities. With extreme reluctance he prepared himself for wedlock. As he could not be expected to pay two rents, my grandfather had taken the precautionary measure of moving to another rented cottage. My great-uncle had stayed on at Model Cottage. The mother gave birth, but before my great-uncle had gathered together his full reserve of courage which would lead him to the altar, the baby died. The idyll was over. It speaks well for my great-uncle, that full support, both moral and financial had been given throughout. So efficiently was a veil cast over the episode that never a whisper had come my way, never one chance remark which would have given me a clue, through all those years.

Some fifteen to twenty years later, my mother was still entertaining, my great-uncle still in the background, more resentful of intrusion than ever, his distaste for visitors all the more exacerbated by nostalgic memories of Miss Elsie West. Now I had appeared, seated restlessly at the table, making mental notes of everything that went on.

Sundays were rarely good days for me, for apart from the tedium of church and Sunday School, I had to remain dressed up. Roamings and explorations of dykes and the edges of ponds were out of the question. Once at Grammar School, there was usually some homework to be completed, ready for the next day. Little wonder that on Sundays I copied my great-uncle's irascibility. The evenings were particularly boring, I remember, with only a cold supper to lighten the darkness.

With the guests assembled for tea, my great-uncle would mutter unkind asides to himself about 'finery' and 'fine talk' and would even indulge in spiteful mimicry. My mother, all too aware of his erant bad manners, would be assembling her anger whilst she entertained at table, ready to pour it over my great-uncle as soon as her 'company' were out of sight.

Miss Annie James of Toulbrick Farm, who was about my age, with her guardian, Miss Ada Lytham, received the full treatment on one Sunday; whilst on another would come Miss Irene Baxter of Bryar's Farm, Lea, Near Preston. She was five years my junior and would be chaperoned by her aunt, Miss Gladys Baxter. Both girls had lost their mothers when they were very young.

How did I entertain these diminutive young people of the opposite sex. I can only hope that I was civil to them, more civil than my great-uncle, although I think he did treat Miss Lytham more tolerably than he did most. Did I bore them with my Meccano set, my collection of cigarette cards and visits to my shoal of fish in my lily-pond?

I have varied recollections of return visits with inviting dollops of jellies, trifles and sweetmeats anticipated for days in advance (food alleviated the misery of Sundays) and of visits to see and fondle favourite animals on both farms.

The Cow

AS I look up from my writing on this last day of October an autumnal gale is blowing and the leaves, now yellowed and browned are swirling about and collecting in heaps on the road sides. Such a morning as this takes me back to the Harvest Festival at Hambleton church. Chrysanthemums also play a part in my reverie for it was for this celebration, so many years ago, that I was sent to deliver a bunch of chrysanthemums and dropped in, unannounced, on a cow.

Inside the church several earnest and devout ladies, ardent disciples and admirers of the Rev. J. Gornall, were busily occupied in decorating for the Harvest Festival. The church for once in the year had lost its musty, sepulchral odour and smelt of freshly cut plants and greenery and above all, of chrysanthemums. Flowers, vegetables and fruits there were a-plenty. Even the pulpit and the great, imperious eagle on the lectern were festooned, tangible reminders that "seed-time and harvest never faileth". By the altar rails was a miniature cornstack, skilfully constructed down to the thatching on its roof.

There was, of course, a pecking order in the busy band of decorators. I should think that their leader then would be Miss Doris Gregson, the organist, who with her sisters, ran the Village Post Office. The ladies flitted about their work, voices lowered in respect for the sanctity of their surroundings.

I got rid of my flowers as quickly as I could, for to be seen carrying them would have drawn accusations of femininity from my rural friends. I made a detour round the back of the church and went along the path by the stone wall and the chestnut trees. As I walked along the churchyard path the spirit moved me to climb up on to the wall, possibly to see if any conkers remained on the tree. I stood up, precariously, on top of the wall and looked round. There below me a couple of yards away, was a cow. She was unaware of the proximity of a human, and was innocently cropping away at the grass.

At this phase in my development I was manipulated by Hollywood. My efforts to emulate the acrobatic feats of the heroes of the Silver Screen often led me into unpleasant or even dangerous situations. I suppose I could have sued film directors or the owners of the Picture House at Poulton for inciting me to engage in yet another wayward act. As I didn't even know that I was being influenced, the thought never occurred to me.

In true wild-west style I crept stealthily and silently along an overhanging bough. At just the right moment I dropped on the cow. I can assure people who have never committed such an action that the protuberances on a cow's backbone are very hard and uneven. The jolt which I received to the sensitive parts of my body were far more painful than the strain on my hips when my legs were thrust widely apart. The animal I had chosen was wider than it should have been for it was big with calf.

For a moment the world stood still. I was frozen in time, my thin legs stretched to the limits as they straddled the cow's body. I had scarcely time to register my severe discomfort before the cow gave a tremdendous start, threw back her head and bellowed. Almost simultaneously the bellow was answered by another which came from the churchyard side of the wall. Though confused with all the sudden activity (the cow was arching her back and trying to get at me with her horns) I glimpsed the contorted face of the Rev. J. Gornall, which had assumed a very high colour, and which was mouthing at me as I began my headlong gallop. I was surprised that such a seemingly mild and placid gentleman could display such physical manifestations of rage; that he who was so quietly spoken could out-bellow a cow.

I clung on as best I could like a competitor in a rodeo, but there was really nothing that I could hold on to. We only covered about twenty yards before I was flung into a 'cow-clap' and a blackberry bush. The Rev. Gornall met me as I limped towards the gate. It was now that his suspicions were confirmed that I had an affinity with the Devil which he was powerless to exorcise.

A subtle change took place in his attitude towards me which became more marked a couple of years later when he came into his church earlier than he should have done to take his Bible Class and was met by the strains of the latest dance tunes belted out by me on the church organ, when I was in my Reginald Dixon/Tower Ballroom mood. When I came to apply for jobs he gave me favourable enough reports though, with no mention of sacrilegious acts or cows.

When I think of the cow now, the mature me is horrified at the irresponsible, thoughtless and stupid act of that mischevious young devil which was me. The cow could easily have lost her calf; she herself could have died. The farmer would have been entirely right in suing. My poor family would not have known which way to turn. It is an episode of which I cannot be proud, although I still laugh about it. Being country-bred, I should have known better. Although it does not excuse me by saying it, it was the only incident in which I was involved where serious damage to other people's property could have taken place.

On second thoughts, there was one other occasion when I did cause what might be termed malicious damage. It must have been when I was about fourteen, two years after the cow. It was when I popped a firework, one pitch-black night, through the letterbox of an elderly couple who were noted for their austere ways.

The letterbox must have been one of those with a box-like structure built on the inside. The firework, a 'banger' of course, went off in the confined space with enough force to awaken all Market Street. It made me give an extra leap to my stride, even though I was by then some distance away, running for all I was worth.

The Cow

What a tale of woe met my mother on her post-round next morning when she delivered the letters through the charred aperture. The house had just been painted, which made matters worse. Although I escaped detection and nothing could be proved I had the uncomfortable feeling that the finger of suspicion was pointed at me. I expressed surprise, particularly when my own mother was the most sceptical at my avowed innocence.

One could move about the village undetected in those unlit nights. I went through a brief spell when I exchanged gates. I would select two front gates of similar size but of different colour and design, one delapidated, one relatively new, and change them round. To prolong discovery and add piquancy to the mystery, the gates had to be some distance apart, so not a little physical effort was needed. Stealth was all-important, for it would have been considered odd to have been observed walking about with a gate at nine or ten o'clock on a starless winter's night,

Again, my mother would usually be met with protestations from irate householders and would have a hand in solving the puzzle, unknowingly setting right that which her errant son had put wrong.

I would hear all about it as it was recounted to the family, and would feign amusement and admiration for one who could conceive such a rascally act. A gleam of approval would appear in my great-uncle's eye, for it was rumoured that he had been active in creating distractions a few decades earlier. It was said, for instance, that a water-butt had been propped at a suitable angle against a door, so that when the owner answered it in his night-shirt, he was met with a deluge of water and had to spring back to escape injury. His candle would be sure to go out, and his candlestick would be lost in the onslaught. Set against such red-blooded stuff, gates were insignificant.

The services on Harvest Sunday were, to my mind, the best in the church's year. The harvest hymns were more to my liking, telling mainly of the stages through which the growing crops advanced with eventual success in spite of the vagaries of the weather. I did not wish to be reminded during the rest of the year that "Earth's joys grow dim, its glories pass away", when I had still to taste those joys and gain whatever glory there was in store for me. My grandfather's favourite hymn was "How bright those glorious spirits shine". Could he have been attracted to the lines, "Lo, these are they from sufferings great who came to realms of light"?

As one would expect in a country parish the church was filled to overflowing for morning and evening service at harvest-time, to such an extent that additional chairs had to be placed in the aisles. There was an extra service for children in the afternoon, when they bore their offerings to the altar.

The weathered, hard-worked farmers and the farm labourers, taking time off for an hour or two, joined with their wives and families in singing the praises of fulfilment. My grandfather's clear tenor voice rang out from the choir stalls, where he had pride of place.

> *"Come ye thankful people come,*
> *Raise the song of harvest home,*
> *All be safely gathered in*
> *Ere the winter storms begin".*

I identified with these people and the environment; was part of it and of them. I could use a spade and fork; knew how and where the fruits and vegetables on display were grown; knew when they were ready for lifting or picking. The peasant in me reached out to savour satisfaction of autumn and harvest, the culmination of another year's cycle.

The Passing of my Benefactor

AS well as working two or three days at the vicarage, my mother would put on her black dress and white lace apron and cap and wait at table when such dignitaries as the Bishop came for a meal. In the early days of my boyhood, my grandmother was co-opted to help with the cooking. At such times everything took second place.

At the vicarage the best china dinner service and the best cutlery were on display in a room richly furnished. On the white tablecloth with the needle-point lace, rested the dishes chosen to regale "My Lord Bishop". Bread sauce, apple sauce, mint sauce were served in sauceboats of which one at least would be silver.

What rejoicing there was when the Bishop, all aglow already from confirming yet another group of newly-fledged Christians, had remarked favourably on the taste and texture of the bread sauce, the gastronomic dream which was my mother's trifle laced with sherry.

Rarely resting, rarely having time to rest, my mother spent another two or three days of her week at Rawcliffe Lodge, attending to the needs of Mrs. Winder. Mrs. Winder lived almost in isolation in a great mansion of a place, Edwardian I fancy, which was not far from the River Wyre and which was approached from a lonely side road. Still not content, my mother was the village post lady. She turned out every morning at about half past seven to sort the letters which had come from Blackpool. Then she shouldered her postbag, mounted her bicycle and set out on her round of delivery. It took her two hours or so, according to the amount of mail she had to handle, for she had to go quite a way outside the village proper. Furthermore, she herself was a source of news, was greeted warmly by the inquisitive. It was not unknown for her to step inside for a drink of tea and a slice of buttered toast. (Both my grandmother and my mother, as stated previously, were so inveterate in their tea-drinking that had tea been considered a drug, they would have been registered as addicts). If my mother was a little late in completing her round, both Mrs. Gornall and Mrs. Winder were tolerant towards her, for they knew that she would make up her time for them by working on into the evenings.

My mother revelled in work. Though she was quite short in stature, she was well-made with well-rounded arms and a very strong constitution. I think that she loved best to cycle along the country lanes between the tall hedges, which were not trimmed back nearly as much as they are now. If there is a choice in the hereafter, she will be pedalling along in the clear morning air, hopefully in her own time continuum of the early 1930s, surrounded by birdsong (she delighted in the sound of birds) with now and then the slow, soothing clip-clop of horse's hoofs and the trundling of a farm-cart.

Grandfather singing in the choir, mother closely associated with the vicarage, how could I escape. It was Sunday School for me and at least the morning service. I sat uneasily with the other gauche youths in the pews at the back near the vestry door. Sometimes our restlessness drew stern reproof from the pulpit when the Rev. Gornall would look fixedly over his spectacles in our direction. It was said that our vicar was a competent theologian but I never reached a stage of advancement when I was able to judge. The sermons vibrated in the air above me and wasted their wisdom on the wall behind.

What with church on Sunday and homework during the week I led a full enough life. On top of everything else I had my piano practice which makes me wonder how I managed my solitary expeditions in the countryside and why they are so predominant. I marvel nowadays at the amount of different skills and enterprises which quite young children can pack into a day, and wonder at their endurance. Yet, looking back, I led just as hectic a life without being aware of feeling abnormally stretched.

As my teens advanced, when I was in about my fourteenth year I took more and more to making trips to the River on my own.

My grandfather had died two years before. To be exact it was the 21st November, 1932. He was seventy-one. During the Spring he had caught a chill which had turned to pleurisy. He had fought the illness successfully, which indicated that for a man turned seventy he still had some inner reserve of strength. During his convalescence, however, instead of improving, his condition began to worsen. He was sent to the Royal Infirmary

My Grandfather in his Church going suit, circa 1930.

at Preston. As I have said already, to be admitted to hospital was an ominous step, for in such institutions, commendable and necessary though they were, old ideas died hard.

My grandfather must have slept away from home when he was a young man, before he married. He and his brother went up into the fells for a 'hay month'. The slopes of the Pennines, the fells as my grandfather called them, were easily visible on a clear day. The two experts wielded their scythes day after day until the meadow-grass on the slopes had been cut. Then they picked up their wages and set off on foot on the long trek home, carrying their scythes with them.

It was a long time ago. He who had swung his scythe with such ease, revelling in his strength and young manhood, was now very sick. His anxious disposition did not allow him to accept his present situation. All he could think of was to get home, even if it was only to die. I had the opportunity to visit him only once. In the marble hall of a ward, an ice palace of cold, menacing silences, smelling of disinfectant, lay encased the immobile form of my grandfather, under spotless linen with never a crease. It was as if he, and all other denizens of this sombre place were laid out for inspection. In my grandfather's eyes was the frightened look of an animal entrapped, with no hope of escape.

In due course he came home but he was in very poor shape, and thus he lingered throughout the summer, moving from his bed which had been set up in a corner of the kitchen to a camp bed under an awning in the garden, when the weather permitted. People were kind. He had as many visitors as he could manage, including the Rev. Gornall who came frequently to see him.

His guardian angel, however, was a bright, active little lady called Mrs. Lydia Melling, who was closely related to the Eaves' family. She was, I think, aunt to Annie Eaves, one of my playmates when I was younger.

Mrs. Lydia Melling was a truly good person, one of the very few people I have known who practised kindness without seeking any reward. She genuinely wished to relieve suffering and alleviate sorrow without seeking any acclaim for herself, without any suggestion of self-gratification. She was Hambleton's very own Sister Theresa, and I for one will remember her as such.

Having been a nurse, she tended my grandfather with professional skill. Come rain or shine, she walked up the Village with her dressings and ointments and would accept not a penny in payment. She and my grandfather were both practising Christians, but whereas one was a member of the Congregational Church which had many followers in Hambleton, the other was Church of England. There was supposed to be unfriendly opposition between the two sects. If there was, none was shown in our house.

Undoubtedly there had been a marked rivalry between the different religious factions in the nineteenth century, which spilled over into the next. The nonconformists — Congregationalists and Methodists — were opposed to alcohol, for instance, a limitation which those in the Church of England who liked a drink tended to mock.

In spite of the care bestowed upon him, my grandfather wasted away slowly, and became ever more weak. Finally, his strong heart gave out and he died on a Monday morning shortly after I had gone to school. My Uncle Ben was with him when he died and had just finished shaving him.

His bearers carried his coffin shoulder high in relays down Market Street and up Church Lane. He was interred at Hambleton Church on 24th November, 1932. The card printed for his burial simply read:-

"In Loving Memory of John, the beloved husband of Elizabeth Bowman".

It added that he had been

"A Faithful Member of the Church Choir for 49 years".

Without my grandfather's wage we were reduced quite considerably as we had to rely mainly on what my mother brought in. Doubtless my Uncle Ben gave what he could until the time that he himself married. My great-uncle must have contributed something, although I never knew how much. It was fortunate that my mother was strong and courageous, for without her we would have been in a sorry plight.

I was feeling more and more insecure as I grew up; becoming more and more aware of responsibilities, fears, problems, worries and sad misfortunes which are the burdens and inheritances of adults. At the moment there was very little I could do to help, except with the garden. My mother was adamant that I should stay at school after the statutory school-leaving age which was fourteen.

In most families there was a father-figure (although in one or two instances I could mention they might have been better without him), and I could not avoid noticing the firm and authoritative security which such a presence gave. I tried to put the circumstances of my birth out of my mind as much as I could. I never revealed or discussed it with my school fellows at Baines, and was cautious in my choice of guests from across the River. If anyone knew about my secret it was never mentioned, nor was I ever taunted with the stigma of being born out of wedlock by any of the villagers.

My lone excursions to the River were brief interludes of escapism from unsettling thoughts and visions of impending uncertainty about what the future had in store.

The River

FOR quite a long stretch the River Wyre is tidal. The tide surges past Preesall, Stalmine, Staynall and Hambleton on the north bank, right up past Shard Bridge to where the River narrows in the upper part of Out Rawcliffe. The tidal flow may even reach the bridge at St. Michaels, a distance of twenty-odd miles, at certain times of the year.

Opposite Hambleton, at full time, the River must be four or five-hundred yards wide; whilst at low tide there is only a stream which can (or could) be forded quite easily by wading. At certain times of the year, high tides such as the 'Spring tides' still cause older inhabitants like my Uncle Ben to turn uneasily in their beds for fear of a watery invasion. Shard Bridge, a toll bridge still, was constructed between 1862-1864, about the time that both my grandfather and my grandmother were born. The 'Cop' was built a little while afterwards, by a philanthropic gentleman called Major Gaskell who presumably farmed Banks Farm.

The Cop was raised up to remove, or at least to reduce to a minimum, the risk of flooding. It is, or was at the time of which I write, a great bank about a quarter of a mile long, at least a dozen feet high, about thirty feet wide at the bottom, tapering to twelve to fifteen feet wide at the top.

The Cop is approached from the main road by one of two tracks. Where these tracks converge were originally two cottages, one brick and one white-washed and thatched. They would have been inhabited by fishermen. In these two dwellings prior to the turn of the century lived two contentious females, Peg and Prue, who, if what has been handed down is true, engaged in a continuous slanging match against each other which sometimes led them to gain more

119

publicity than they sought. One cannot but speculate whether one of these contestants left her mark on a place a little way along the Cop, where the sluice-gate regulates the flow of the water from the marsh and prevents the tide from getting through. It is called Peg's Pool.

One cottage has gone. The other has been transformed beyond all recognition into an edifice which now dominates the river from this point. The site is called Bunker's Hill.

On a hot day, with no wind or only a slight breeze blowing, the sun can be quite penetrating out on the marshes, and the prospect serene and beautiful. But on a dour day, with a chill in the air and the prevailing wind lashing in from the Irish Sea, only the hardiest folk will relish the exposure.

If one prefers to wallow in lukewarm water, or take a gentle swim one should seek the placid beaches of the Eastern Mediterranean. The River Wyre is obviously far more daunting because of its geographical position, which ensures that the temperature of the water is never more than just bearable to most. There are also currents and eddies which can never be ignored. When the tide is running strongly over muddy stretches (and it comes in fast), the water becomes disturbed and murky. The River was my friend in much the same way that I might choose a bull for a friend. Most of the time it would accept me, but vigilance remained uppermost, because there was always the chance that it might turn against me. The element of danger must have appealed, for I found the visits to Cocker Street Baths in Blackpool less and less attractive. I must have been something of a masochist too, for I loved to feel the tingle of the salt on my body as I ran along the water's edge to dry myself in the wind.

One of my first memories of the River, when I was about ten, before I ever thought of entering it, was of a frame-like structure erected on the bend opposite Skippool, which was on the other bank. At low tide it stood out on the sandbanks and there were nets on it. I was told that this was where salmon were caught.

Before my time, even during my boyhood there were still salmon, though sadly depleted in number. During the Great War, my great-uncle was still able to "prick for flukes" successfully. These 'flukes' were plaice or flounders which burrowed into the sandy bed of the river. My great-uncle would collect buckets full of these flukes by pricking them out with a metal-tined rake. Salted and dried in late summer or early autumn they formed a staple part of the diet in the hard days of scarcity in winter.

The river offered a delicacy much favoured by some. There was a big 'mussel-skier' or 'skeer' near Wardleys where the mussels multiplied. It was still there in 1935 as I knew to my cost when I picked my way through it with my bare feet. By then the mussels must have deteriorated in quality.

Formerly, they had been raked up off the pebbles and stones to which they had clung and had been taken a little way down river to 'Staynall Hole' and laid down again. There they were allowed to grow and mature for two more years before they were disturbed. So popular were these shellfish that rough-hewn men with long narrow carts made special journeys from Preston to transport the half-hundredweight bags, still dripping with sea-water, back to the market there, where they were sold as Hambleton Hookings. Apparently there was also an oyster bed opposite, on the other bank.

There was also a marsh plant called 'sandforth' or 'sanforth' which was collected and sold from house to house. In Hambleton it was not as prolific or of as good a qaulity as it was nearer the estuary.

When Hambleton was but a few houses and Wardleys saw the tall masts of sea-going ships berthed there, the natives must have relied upon the river to assist in keeping them alive. There were 'flukes' and salmon and there must have been other fish too; there were oyster, mussels and sandforth. I deduce that a major change began during the First World War and there was a marked deterioration. I do not profess to understand marine biology but the reason which springs first to mind is pollution. Fortunately, at about the same time more efficient transport began to deliver cheap fresh fish from Fleetwood and even futher afield.

To return briefly to Wardleys and the tall ships. I have heard it said that Wardleys was a thriving port visited by vessels from as far away as Russia, but this had been long before my time. The only indication of its former status was the big warehouse in which such cargoes as tallow and timber had been stored.

My grandmother, protesting about the untidiness of her kitchen when it did not meet her scrupulous demands, would say that it was like "a padding-can". The word is 'padding-ken', and the dictionary definition is "a low lodging-house inhabited by thieves". Such places had existed in Hambleton. If they had not been patronised by thieves in the strict sense, they would have housed some very dubious characters. One could visualise the crews of the ships in port storming ashore to fill themselves with grog at Wardleys Hotel or the Shovels Inn before they rampaged through the village seeking lodgings. There would be a few anxious husbands and fathers fearful for the safety of wives and daughters, though a few wayward wenches would be attracted as always to reckless men of the sea from foreign parts. Hard as it was to imagine in the placid 1930s, there must have been some wild goings-on, with raucous voices carrying on the night air, and screams and fleeing feet and the flurry of women's skirts.

Nearer my own time, but not near enough, when my great-uncle was a young man, he and a couple of confederates of similar mind had conceived what they considered to be yet another diversion to while away a long winter's evening. There was still a lodging-house which stood approximately across the road from Sunderlands Farm, across from the junction of Sunderlands Lane and Market Street. Barrows filled with manure from the farm's midden were wheeled across the road and tipped and spread along the patch and across the door-step of the lodging-house.

Part of Sunderlands Farm, circa 1903. It was pulled down in the 1900's to make way for a modern structure.

Naturally, great caution was needed. Knowing my great-uncle, one could be sure that only the ripest and most offensive manure would be chosen and spread. My great-uncle's gang, having laid the trap, would take cover and wait for the unwary lodgers to return, and watch them slip and fall about on the rich carpet which had been prepared especially for their arrival. The hidden watchers would be greatly amused at the consternation caused, their glee further enhanced by the impressive flow of invective which the incident provoked.

Murmurs of furtive, unheralded visits by intruders of a more sinister kind had also filtered down from the distance of nearly one and a half centuries. Shadowy figures had emerged at night from the mists of the river and had swooped unsuspected and unannounced on innocents, crouched over the fire with their clay-pipes and mugs of ale in one of the two hostelries, at the end of the day's labours.

These poor unfortunates had been spirited away to serve in His Britannic Majesty's Navy during the Napoleonic Wars.

One of these was James Thompson of the same strain as that Alice Thompson, my great-grandmother, whose name had been bequeathed to my mother. This James Thompson, "as broad as he was long" in appearance had lived to come safe home. Said to have been the first to board a French ship at Trafalgar he was rewarded with 'spade-ace' guineas, enough to fill his wide-brimmed sailor's hat. It was also said that this prize money was tranferred to a 'piggin' or wooden cow-trough and hidden in a farm building. What happened to it subsequently was never revealed.

Now, in 1988, only one small section of the warehouse wall is left to remind me of Wardleys as a bustling, thriving productive community. Across an expanse of concrete which is the car-park, Wardleys Hotel still stands. No longer white-washed it has been dressed in colours considered more appropriate to attract today's society. No longer a haven for sea-farers and fisher folk it has become a pleasure-palace for its cossetted customers of the late twentieth century.

Between the Clough and the Hotel, by the road along which my great-uncle made his nightly perambulations, today's mariners assemble, owners of the small craft in which they play their game of sailoring. Like Marie Antoinette with her model farm at Petit Trianon and her stylish milk-maid's gown, these modern sailors with plenty of leisure indulge their fancy to imitate their predecessors who struggled so fiercely to make a living from the sea.

I would have liked to have indulged a fancy that my great-uncle's spirit would still travel this route, once so familiar to him. I fear that it will not. He is gone forever and with him his hardy, individualistic contemporaries. It is as well. My great-uncle, scornful enough of the changes about him in his own life-time would find nothing to commend, everything to deride and would expire anew, choked by a fit of contemptuous ridicule.

The salmon in the river in the 1930s must have been so

few as to be negligible. The trade in Hambleton Hookings
had gone; the Hookings themselves had dwindled. Very few
flukes were caught and these were more often too small for
consumption. Sometimes when wading over sandy beds in
the channel I would feel something wriggle under my feet.
I knew they were flukes but they were never more than six
inches long.

It was said that there were quicksands, especially in the
area where I had seen the salmon nets. I loitered in this
area often enough, kicking about in the coarse sand. I may
have been lucky, but all I ever felt was suction in places if
I stood still. I did, however, get bogged down in the stiff,
clinging mud just off Skippool, to such an extent that I sank
to beyond my knees. I never went there again.

There was one whole year (about 1936) when I took my
costume and towel and sped down the Village on every
possible opportunity to take my dip in the River. My aim
was never to miss a day. Although there were some days
when I must have failed, there were not many. Whatever
the weather, whatever the state of the tide, I found somewhere to submerge myself even if I couldn't have a good
swim. Quite often I did not use my towel. Like my great-
uncle before me, I believed in the beneficial property of
dried salt on my skin. As I have related in the incident with
Little Joe, I braved snowstorms and sleet, as well as roar-
ing winds. It was exhilarating to be alone out there on the
fringe of darkness with the tide rushing in and a gale
blowing.

Peg's Pool was known to me as the 'Cut'. It is a deep ditch
or channel running from the 'Cop' to the river. When the
tide is up, the Cut is filled with water and will be at least
fifteen feet wide and about twelve feet deep. It was probably dug, or cut out about the same time as the Cop was
thrown up.

The Cut was not the most hygienic or safest of places in
which to swim. Old bicycle frames and perambulators
found a last resting place there. Round the trap-door or
sluice-gate a strong concrete emplacement had been built

into the Cop. It formed a natural platform from which I could dive, when the tide was up. I had to endure the flotsam and jetsam which gathered there, and even effluence at times. Hidden underwater hazards had to be avoided. If I were asked to take a header from the concrete base now, I should run the other way. The possibility of encountering sharp bicycle spokes would frighten me.

My custom was to dive out as far as I could and to swim as far as I could underwater, using my hands to detect obstacles, for it would have been foolhardy of me to open my eyes. One fine Saturday afternoon in summer conditions were just right. The water was relatively clear. I practised my routine in leisurely fashion, sunbathed for a while, then in carefree mood went home in search of some tea. Up the Village consternation reigned. Old Mr. Jackson, surrounded by a couple of his relatives, stood transfixed at his garden gate as he saw me approaching. I was regarded as if I were an apparition and was greeted guardedly, as if there might be no reply.

It turned out that Mr. Jackson had observed my activity at the Cut, had seen me plunge in but had not seen me come out. Thinking that I had drowned, he hastened homewards as fast as he was able, not assisting his health in the process, in order to raise the alarm. A debate had just started on who was to be the bearer of the sad news to my family. My timely transition from the dead to the living made such a visit superfluous. The news soon spread, nevertheless, causing me further harassment at home and a good deal of persuasive reassurance on my part on the safety of my actions.

There was one afternoon, never-to-be-forgotten, when I settled myself down and prepared to die, uncomforted and all alone. I lay in the summer grass under the hedge on top of the bank overlooking the spot where the salmon-frame had been. It was ironic, I though, that I had to depart on such a fine day — and I so young.

I had been idling about in the River, turning over and over in the sunlit water in imitation of a porpoise or a seal, when a searing pain shot up my leg from ankle to knee. So severe was the pain that I gasped and cried out. There was no one within at least half-a-mile to hear me. I swam to the shallow water as best I could and stumbled over the flat stretch of sand and soggy marshland and up the bank to seek cover. For the first time in my life I felt weak and unsteady. I was sure that I was dying when my vision became blurred.

My leg was swollen and covered in blotches and it had stiffened up, making movement difficult. I daren't go home, for a couple of hours could not have got home. Had it happened today I might have tried to drag myself to Shard Bridge, where a passing motorist would summon an ambulance. If there were such vehicles organised to answer emergency calls to outlying districts in those days, the round trip would have taken two hours.

Slowly the pain abated and the swelling had reached its peak. When the sun told me it was late afternoon, I went down to where I had left my clothes, dressed myself and walked slowly home. As I was feeling better I never told anyone. My long trousers hid my leg, which remained swollen and discoloured for a few more days. It was so uncharacteristic of me not to attack my meals with my customary enthusiasm that my grandmother was heard to ask if "Our Ed was badly"?

Not having sought medical advice and therefore not having had any opinion on the cause, I always assumed that I had been stung by a monster jellyfish. I still went back to the River.

As an afterthought I have decided to add one final comment to the chapter. There was living in Hambleton a newcomer, extraordinary in that he was an expert swimmer. He encouraged me and latterly accompanied me to the River. His name was Les MacNeil. It was he who gave me the confidence to swim across the River and back at full tide, swept along in places by the strong currents; it was he who escorted me like a pilot-vessel whilst I did so. He was a big, fine, friendly fellow. He had many friends himself.

WHEN EVERY DAY WAS SUMMER

They were all very sorry to hear of his death whilst he was serving abroad with the Royal Air Force, shortly after the Second World War.

Land Hill Farm

I CANNOT estimate with any certainty when it was that I first went to Land Hill Farm and met the residents there. My first memory is of going to seek permission to visit from my grandfather who was working down Paul Street on a Saturday morning. He was reluctant at first, being cautious, and thought that I was too young and might come to some harm. I suppose I must have been about eight or nine. There must have been a member of the Land Hill family present and willing to take me, for I would not have been allowed to make the journey on my own.

The farm was across the fields, about a mile as the crow flies but almost twice that distance by road. The normal route was up Church Lane, past the church and left at the T-junction at Bickerstaff, that area held in much respect by my Great-uncle Dick for its supernatural aura and visitations. Over half-a-mile further on, passing two or three farms on the way, another farm could be seen, sitting some distance up a cart track on the left- hand side.

A long frontage of farmhouse and farm buildings was presented, with a perimeter fence of hedges, with tall trees and orchards set within.

Having travelled beyond the gate from the main road, a barrier always kept closed to prevent cattle from straying, the track led to another gate from which the farmyard could be seen. It was like a mediaeval courtyard, surrounded on three sides by buildings — stable, shippons, pigsty and barn.

In former days the farmstead had been designed and laid out, not only as a means of support, but also as a haven where the delights of nature could be contemplated and enjoyed.

Across the yard was a pond, stagnant and polluted by seepage from faulty drains from the buildings. Time was, it was said, that this pond had been ornamental and stocked with colourful fishes. Trees had been planted to afford shade as well as decoration. They had grown out-of-hand over the years or had decayed and fallen into the water. There were still signs of flowerbeds and paths edged with glazed tiles. Beyond the pond was a large greenhouse which in former days had been a showpiece in itself. Beside it was a tiny dilapidated cottage. Who dwelt in this lonely idyllic spot? Was it a coachman or gardener, or one person serving for both? Or had it lodged a dissolute, mutilated or deformed member of the family who had to be kept permanently away from the public gaze? There was still a tiny kitchen range, falling away to rust. The one downstairs room now housed an incubator in which eggs were hatched out during a few weeks in the year.

Looking at that small, rectangular incubator for the first time, noting with interest that it was heated with an oil lamp, that the control of an even temperature needed constant care and skill, watching the chicks cracking their shells and emerging, with plenty of room to move about, how could I have possibly foreseen that fifty or sixty years later electrically-heated and thermostatically controlled devices, built on a huge scale, would produce thousands of chicks at a time, one batch succeeding another in hypnotic succession.

Land Hill's output, tiny golden bundles at first, would be of just sufficient number to re-stock the cabins and would spend their useful lives in natural surroundings, some pecking about near the midden or stack-yard, or round the back door of the farmhouse. Those later ones of a new age would be destined to meet the needs of an increased population eager to devour chicken at every meal and to consume mountains of eggs for their health-giving properties. Cramped in prisons two or three to a cell, the hens would battle and fight and damage each other, laying all the time with machine-like efficiency, until, their usefulness over

130

they would end up hung upside down on hooks on an endless line, just as their younger sisters and brothers had done which had been reared and grown scientifically and as quickly as possible — purely for food.

The Land Hill poultry were just about economically viable, the emphasis still being on self-sufficiency with something over to meet costs and labour, and a little bit over, with luck, rather than on factory farming with enormous profits (after a huge initial outlay), worked out to the last decimal point.

In the chicken farms of the future, trained staff, white-coated, wearing different coloured hats denoting status or standard of efficiency, would dismantle the chain of corpses, mile after mile of them. These chicken surgeons would be so skilful, so carefully trained that there was the very minimum of waste. The most horrifying and abhorrent aspects, to the observer, would be the way in which directors and management would manipulate the workforce through competition and reward to enjoy their macabre calling, to become impervious to extermination on a massive scale.

What would be difficult to comprehend would be the sheer size of such enterprises; with every indication that they would grow bigger and bigger until they assumed nightmare proportions, until some great catastrophe resulted in an abrupt reversion. After which, mankind, still retaining its unique characteristic for never being satisfied with status quo, a characteristic which other living creatures do not possess, would commence its slow, relentless climb back to the chicken farm.

To return to a tour of the farm, still tranquil, still undisturbed by even a ripple of industrial intrusion, there were all the signs of money once having been spent for a gentleman's indulgence. With a change of ownership less well endowed, there had been a slow and relentless disregard for general maintenance. Nature had become less controlled. In brickwork in woodwork there were ominous signs of decay. Paint had peeled off doors blistered by sun and by ravages of winters' gales and was never replaced during the years of my association. Lethargy, or was it apathy, was the overriding feeling.

The Bowman breed, family or clan, call it what you will, was insular. The men cared little for social visits either between themselves or between anyone else. Tea parties and other sit-down meals such as christenings or weddings were barely tolerable. Even at Christmas they might show restraint in attitude. The women-folk were more relaxed and the noticeable reluctance for social interchange did not apply at all to those who had entered the family by marriage.

At Land Hill Farm the clan Bowman reigned supreme. Everyone carried this surname, so when I joined it I entered its domain without question or censure. The 'portcullis' was raised, the 'drawbridge' lowered.

The Bowmans, living in the isolation they chose and demanded, with no encouragement given to would-be intruders, were akin to the Doones, but with the aggression excluded.

The farm was owned by my grandfather's brother, Jonathan. He lived in Hambleton and owned a large detached house called West Lodge, which stood in its own exclusive grounds. Where my Great-uncle Jonathan's residence was, shops now stand.

Great-uncle Jonathan (I called him uncle) walked over the hill and across the fields from Hambleton nearly every day. His arrival could always be anticipated if there was a special need for subterfuge, for the approaches to his outlying property were under observation, whichever way he chose to come. He was still a commanding figure, tall and well-made, though he walked with a stick. By virtue of his dominance he had been the most successful in business of the four brothers. His shrewdness was not to be despised. Apart from holding the purse-strings very tightly, his presence must have contained a certain hidden menace as well as authority, for though on the surface he was disarming enough and quietly spoken, tension was in the air when he was about.

When I started my visits, the other brother, Dick, the boggart-ridden one, lived and worked on the farm. His job was really a sinecure, for he had become slow and feeble. Soon he was to join his brother Ben, who lived with Jonathan at headquarters in the big house in the village. There he was to decline further and then die. As far as I can remember, he was a gentle, kindly old man, totally devoid of malice. He was thin to the point of emaciation. Dick had never married. In former days it was he who had taken up his scythe with my grandfather and stepped out for his hay-month in the fells; had played the piccolo and the fiddle to the accompaniment of my grandfather's cello.

In a much earlier age he might have been found as a lay-brother tending bees or cultivating herbs in the garden of some secluded monastic settlement; might even have risen to a desk in the cloisters, illuminating manuscripts.

These were old men of whom I write, their ambitions, interests, zest and enthusiasm all gone — or nearly so. Great-uncle Ben of the huge frame now much stooped, of the giant's hands which could be manipulated to create with sensitivity, still managed to cultivate a kitchen-garden at West Lodge, in spite of his chronic rheumatism. His remaining passion was for producing a bed of large onions. This somewhat unusual urge fell briefly on one or the other through two generations until behold, half-a-century later it came to rest on me.

Stanley, another Bowman of course, also worked on the farm but had married recently, and lived in the Village. He was Jonathan's son and was in some respects a much younger Dick. Though quietly spoken and inoffensive to most, he was like those others who surrounded me in that he was adept at segregating flaws, faults and what he considered to be objectionable qualities. Ostentation and affectation were particularly vulnerable to the fire of his wry humour, which was not free from cynicism. Never once did he treat me with anything but kindliness and courtesy.

Again it was from hearsay that I gathered that he was a good pianist; though I came too late to hear him play.

The occupant, farmer and person in charge was Tom Bowman, another of Jonathan's sons. He stood well over six feet, was big-boned and very lean. His hair was red, now tinged with white, and he had a clipped moustache to match. A long face added strength to his appearance. Like my great-uncle he refrained from shaving for three or four days at a stretch. The red bristles, never allowed to develop into a beard, made him appear quite formidable. He could look fixedly at anyone with his piercing eyes without any sign of flinching. When he applied this technique it was daunting on its own. Apart from size there were several qualities in appearance and in behaviour which were common to Tom of Land Hill and Tom my great-uncle. Handsome in a rugged way, striking in manner and physique, this Tom would not have looked out of place, one imagined, as a member of a Viking horde employed in flaying a group of unfortunate monks and nailing their skins to church doors. He had taken boxing lessons earlier in life and he would sometimes encourage me to indulge in playful bouts. When he pushed out his long, wiry arms, covered in red fur, he transmitted strength, as if he were charged with some powerful electric current.

Tom Bowman of Land Hill Farm, about 1920.

Like my grandfather, he was not adverse to a chew of tobacco, as a change from his cigarettes. Like my grandmother, Tom's wife was opposed to the habit. But whereas my grandmother's protests were shrill, her's were administered quietly.

Tom possessed the same shrewd observation, the same cynical, wry humour and wit as the other members of his family. He was, however, inclined to be more impish in his actions and more scathing in his comments.

There is one story which reveals his waggish nature. When Tom had been one of the young gallants of the village, seeking diversions as young men do after work was done, there had been a fire, somewhere in the region of the Reading Room. It must have been quite an event for the local policeman had been summoned to supervise. Whether there was a fire-engine on the scene, whether there was indeed a fire-engine to call upon is not revealed. There was certainly no such machine housed in Hambleton. What is known is that buckets were being used, either solely or as supplementary aids, to put out the blaze. Tom was one of the bucket-bearers, an enthusiastic helper working in the darkness. Instead of pouring the water over the blaze he contrived to pour it over the policeman's boots, each time making some trivial comment by way of diversion. The policeman was engrossed in the activity of putting out the fire and must have had that sort of mind which could only concentrate on one thing at a time. He was heard to comment from time to time that his feet were cold. It was in the depths of winter, freezing hard, for when the static guardian of peace came to move his extremities, not only had he lost all feeling in them but he found that they were frozen solid to the ground.

There is another tale about Tom, for which veracity my Uncle Ben must be responsible. It reveals the danger, for the most part latent, which lay in this man. One can only speculate on the scene presented, not knowing all the facts, but the finale was abrupt and to one at least, memorable.

A Conservative meeting, probably held at Hambleton Reading Room, had ended and the politically-motivated were making their exit, well wrapped-up against the cold, for the ground was covered in a thick blanket of snow. There must have been some heated exchanges which promoted the swift and belligerent act which was to finish the debate for good and all. One gentleman, who had acquired the pseudonym 'Mutton', was particularly vociferous. His manner and the content of his argument must have rankled particularly with Tom. Tom may not have had a lot to say, not caring much for the power of verbal persuasion. He was busily stamping a 'patten', building up a solid block of snow with his foot.

A patten is defined as "a wooden sole with an iron ring, worn under the shoe to keep it from the wet". Ladies wore this device to lift them from the mire, and from the manure which strewed the roads.

Tom, unremarked by his companions, certainly unremarked by Mutton, was not to be satisfied with his patten until it was big enough and hard enough for his purpose. When it was he reached down, took it in his great hairy hand and hurled it at Mutton with considerable force, striking him full in the mouth. Muttons' outburst ended on the impact, his flow of words cut-off in mid- stream. It was one decisive way of ending a political argument, a way which did not encourage freedom of speech.

Margaret was Tom's wife. There was over a dozen years difference between them, so she was appreciably younger than her husband. They were a good match for all that. If they ever fell out they were careful to keep it between themselves. Still only in her late twenties she was small, pretty and vivacious. Margeret loved dancing and was as light as a feather on her feet. she had a versatile singing voice and could produce a very creditable imitation of Gracie Fields, her greatest idol. The glamour of the theatre attracted her, as did the cinema and its growing array of stars. Being of a different strain from the introvert Bowmans, on to which stock she had been grafted, she did not altogether accept the insularity which was synonymous with living at Land Hill, although she put on a brave front and was rarely anything but cheerful. She usually managed to visit Blackpool once a week. This was quite a journey, first on bicycle or on foot, then by Ribble bus. Once in a while she went away on holiday for a few days, leaving the men-folk to fend for themselves in spartan style.

It may well be wondered why I, a lad still at Hambleton Council School, should be eager to mingle with a body of adults of such mixed age-groups. The reason was not to be found in them, but in the companionship of Arthur, Tom and Margaret's only child.

Arthur, splendidly and impressively christened Thomas Arthur Lord Bowman, was a lively young fellow, a year or so younger than I, who had inherited not only his father's red hair but much of his temperament.

Whilst I had already formed associations in the village Arthur had been reared in his own fortress and had learnt to create and enjoy his own solitary pleasures within the confines of its ramparts. His friend was his dog, a savage enough beast to others, but utterly compliant to him. Even now he was managing to handle work-horses. There was one called Jack with whom he had a special understanding

Margaret, Tom's wife, with son Arthur, taken in 1920's.

and who did not display to him the bad temper he showed to grown-ups.

Through enforced seclusion from his peers, through constant contact with older people, themselves always ready to question or to contradict orthodox thought, he was already at this early age on the way to being freed from the restrictions imposed by the herd.

When I became Arthur's playmate and entered his very own private reserve another important diversion was superimposed; another distraction was added to those previously described. My Latin and French, my English and Maths and certainly my Chemistry were soon to suffer some further neglect because of the carefreee indulgences which lay within the hedges which formed the boundaries of Land Hill Farm.

Ned Was a Good Milker

PEERING into the past from a distance of over fifty
years, I am struggling to assess what particular lure
there was at Land Hill, which a the time transcended
all other. Could it have been that Arthur and I formed a
close friendship which family ties made even more secure?
As we grew up the bonds grew even closer. There was
period when we were inseparable. We laughed a lot and
were not very gallant in that we made pointed references to
the weaknesses of acquaintances in the district, or pilloried
them when they were not present to hear them and to
defend themselves. We had our own special communication
signal. It was a high-pitched yodel which we sent ringing
across the fields and through wooded places and orchards
in order to show where each one was when we were separated.

As for the pursuits which made a day at Land Hill flash
past, they were manifold. What unparalleled joy it was to
awake on a day in the holidays, to realise that I was bound
for the farm. At half-past eight in the morning with the sun
already warming the weathered bricks of the stable-wall
where the sand-pit was, Arthur was already up and about
this hour or two past and was looking for my coming. The
whole day stretched ahead, with brief breaks for meals in
between which were taken as hurriedly as we dared for
there was much to do. Arthur's father and mother, whom
we mutually took to calling 'Pa' and 'Ma', looked indulgent-
ly on us unless propriety had to be observed if a guest was
present.

139

All too soon the evening shadows began to fall, and I was sent off home, in good time before dark. I was tired and dirty, with my face streaked where the sweat had run down, but I was so happy.

In hay-time there were the carts to ride in; the hay-cocks to run between and to tumble over. There were the 'moos' (hay-mows) or 'lofts' where we jumped about on the newly housed hay, and got in everyone's way. It was 'Catteralls' repeated, but in a different setting. In the barn was a wooden barrel of beer, specially delivered to slake the thirst of the hay-makers. When it was thought that we were old enough, we were allowed to take a swallow or two, a very special privilege. The taste must have been to my liking for it has never left me.

There were other enticements which led us to stacks or barns in other seasons. We could always clamber up a ladder and roll about and wrestle in the hay, even if we did end up choking and sneezing with the dust and with the usual collection of unwelcome hay-seeds in our clothing. We burrowed in from the side of the 'rick' in the Dutch barn, which by definition had open sides and a corrugated iron roof, and made our stifled way through to the other side, almost suffocating ourselves by doing so. I was never as keen on this kind of adventure after I saw a rick of corn, which stood alongside the hay, dismantled to be threshed. When the bottom sheaves were thrown up rats scurried about in profusion, many to be pounced on by the dogs who were eager and waiting. The same rats must have been round and about us, monitoring our progress as we burrowed through the hay.

What was work for the men was fun for us. We helped to pick the apples and pears and plums, with dire punishments threatened if we handled the fruit carelessly and damaged it. Whoever had first planted the orchards knew their business. The varieties he had chosen were good, but the yield would have been greater, had regular pruning and spraying been carried out.

When the trees were bare Arthur would rummage about

for an old cart-rope or two. We ran them from one tree to another, thus making our own assault course. Uttering strange cries in the best "Tarzan of the Apes, Johnny Weismüller" tradition, we suspended ourselves by our arms and swung along, using up incredible amounts of energy. Travellers new to the area, passing along the road could not be blamed for thinking that in yonder manorial hall dwelt an eccentric who indulged himself with his own private menagerie. They would, of course, have been right about the eccentric.

I suppose the pleasure I got from Land Hill was spread over several years. As I developed physically and grew more responsible I was drawn into the working life of the farm. Under the disciplined guidance of Tom, who was an expert in a bewildering array of skills, I eventually qualified as a farm servant.

I mixed the food for the hens and took it to the cabins in fields distant from the farm building. I collected the eggs and cleaned out hen-cabins on my own, becoming familiar with the hen-lice which were all too ready to retaliate. During one very hard winter when we were in our mid-teens, Arthur and I took time off between duties and slid on the ponds which were frozen solid. Our clog-irons, or 'cokers' as they were called, acted as runners. Often the ponds were not safe, especially if there were trees overhanging under which the ice was thin.

The grass, hedges and tree-branches glistened, thick with hoar frost. It was indeed a 'winter-wonderland' in which we were privileged to live. The land lay silent about us, with a light mist lying. Nothing moved. No bird sang. The hens, usually foraging far and wide, were glad to be under cover. All the cattle and horses were safely sheltered, warm on their bedding in shippon and stable. Even the donkey, resting from his tour of duty on the sands, though a hardy enough fellow, had been put into a snug corner of some shed or other which happened to be vacant.

WHEN EVERY DAY WAS SUMMER

*"The north wind doth blow, and we shall have
    snow,
And what will the robin do then, poor thing?
He'll sit in the barn, and keep himself warm,
And hide his head under his wing, poor thing".*

I had been taught this on my grandfather's knee. Such
thoughtfulness, common throughout my family was also
shared I suspect, by many if not all country folk. To have
experienced regularly the rigours of exposure must bring
out a special sympathy.

Arthur and I, our hands blue, with no feeling in the
fingers, our ears red and tingling, would ourselves slip into
the shippon. The warm air, impregnated with the odour of
manure surrounded us as we leaned against cows which
were placid enough to accept our cold hands laid upon
them.

* * * *

Tom taught me to milk. He sneered at anyone who did
not attack the teats with vigour. With great, long, strong
pulls he kept the milk flowing into the bucket held firmly
between his legs. He insisted that there must be a continuous stream produced from the two alternating jets of milk,
causing a white foam to build up in the bucket.

In bursts of energy rarely displayed, he treated us to
exhibition bouts in milking. With his long legs braced and
straddled on either side of his short, three-legged milking-
stool, with his bucket firmly clenched and with his head so
tight against the cow's flank that the peak of his stained
cloth cap was tilted sideways, he entered into a frenzy of
rhythmic continuity which set the milk streaming and
frothing. Sweat stood out on his forehead as he showed his
craftsmanship and artistry. I felt humble and inspired in
the presence of such a master. I flung myself at my own cow
with great determination. Arthur was less inspired. Proud
as he was of his father's ability, he hid his true feelings from
me beneath a condescending indulgence for the whims and

eccentricities which to him were everyday events of little consequence.

Indirectly, I was awarded the accolade. Tom mentioned to some acquaintance that "Ned was a good milker". To everyone at Land Hill I was known as Ned. When the comment was passed back to me it pleased me, even if I never overcame the heifer-problem. Heifers, young cows which had recently dropped their first calves, quite often had very little teats. Trying to grip these little rubbery button-like things between fingers and thumb in order to draw off short jets of milk was too tedious a process for me.

I came to like cows and formed an affinity with them, except for a few who were cantankerous. They were just like humans — taking all sorts to make a world. As I watched them make their leisurely way up from the field to be milked on a summer's afternoon, I was interested in their behaviour. Each one knew her own place in the shippon, but not all went straight there. There was the one which blocked the doorway, or tried to force her way past; there was the one which went deliberately to the wrong stall or 'boost' and caused disruption in the flow of 'traffic'. At such times Tom's long arm would reach out very heavily. If there was a milking-stool within reach the wayward cow would be made to blink and would be dissuaded from trying that trick again when Tom was about.

Always there would be one cow which was not above poking at the flank of another with her horns. "Tha mun look out — woo's rather keen at porkin' folk wi' 'er horns". The word horn was also used as a verb: "Oo'll horn thi if th'are not careful" meant, "She'll apply her horns to you if you don't take care".

In contrast there were the timid ones. These were they, who, if they could have assumed human form would have cringed in corners at parties or would have sat in the shadows whilst other more extrovert types would converse loudly and guffaw round and over them. These inoffensive cows would go straight to their places and stand still, looking straight ahead with big, round eyes, whilst they were tied up.

When all the animals were lined up in position we went round and fastened them up by the necks. An anti-social one might lash out as we edged between as there was not much room, or might jerk her head about as the tie-rope was put round.

I felt far more at home with cows, and also with bulls as I shall tell, than I ever did with horses. Horses were not for me. Even Old Tinker, mildest of horses and a veteran of the Great War, with shell splinters just below his hide to prove it, was not above "coming the old soldier". He was soon quelled, however, for like most old soldiers he was surprised and glad to be alive, and was not looking for trouble. Neither of the two horses were big ones like my great-uncle's Shires.

Why is it that all the horses I have met and this included donkeys, have tried to bite me? They always go for the upper arm. Is it something to do with my body sweat, I wonder, or am I just ripe for biting?

My failure to ride the churchyard cow still rankled. My bruises and the admonition by the Rev. Gornall had not been sufficient to put me off, and I welcomed the chance to try again. This came on a fine summer's evening. Arthur and I, considered old enough to be left on our own by now, watched from some hidden spot like two stoats as 'Pa' and 'Ma' wheeled their bicycles out of the bottom gate and rode sedately towards Hambleton, bound for some meeting or other. We went up the field to Stony End Pit (all ponds were pits), where some "young things" had assembled under the trees. These young things, just out of the calf stage, were not quite old enough for the attention of the bull and unlike the churchyard cow, they were not in calf. Yet they were quite sturdy, lean and generally in good trim. Having fed and tended them when they were laid up in calf-pens or loose-boxes in winter, they knew us, so that we could approach them without rousing their suspicion.

We chose our own mounts, grasped them round the necks

and heaved ourselves on board. Being young and frisky, they went hell-for-leather down that field, kicking up their heels behind them. The ride was stimulating, breath-taking in fact. We each lasted for about a hundred yards before we fell off.

This was our last venture of its kind with cattle, not only because of the telling-off we received, for we should have known that unseen watchers were always at work who would be only too ready to report on our mis-deeds, but also because we grew out of cows and such. We rode the horses bareback a few times, but this was not frowned on nearly as much. It goes without saying that I rode Tinker, whilst the more accomplished and assured Arthur pranced about on Jack.

There were incidents with donkeys at Land Hill. The one which springs readily to mind involved a predecessor of he for whom shelter had been found in a memorable severe winter of the mid 1930s. Arthur, toiling away in a secret place had created a two-wheeled equipage which must have surely been the meanest and most insecure of its kind. The shafts were discarded hen-perches, the body was part of an old door and the wheels had been salvaged from a push-bike. The harness, as far as I remember, was made up of clothes lines which had been discharged from regular service, and the ubiquitous bottling-string. Being only young (nine, ten, eleven?) it was to Arthur's credit that such transport had been constructed at all.

Having manoeuvred the donkey of that year into position between the hen-perches, not without difficulty for this creature contained all the perverse stubborness and reluctance of his kind, and having tied him in, or, as Arthur would say, "geared him up", we climbed on to the super-structure. Arthur, driving of course, gathered his improvised reins, stirred up the donkey's rear quarters with his foot and we lurched away, swaying from side to side and making the most alarming metallic noises as we went. Viewed from a distance, we could have conveyed to a myopic person a brief vision of the mystic East in that our

transport contained shades of aristocratic elegance, sugges-
tive of tongas or rickshaws and guardians of Empire.

Speaking solely for myself, it could not be said that it was
a relaxed outing. I was ill-at-ease, perched up there beside
Arthur who fell far short of being in full control. As with all
donkeys this one had been cute enough to weigh-up the
situation. No matter how manfully the reins were manipulated, the donkey made straight for a hawthorn hedge and
trotted very close to it with one wheel running parallel.
Suddenly, very suddenly, he spotted what he was looking
for. Our conveyance swerved sharply at right-angles and
became wedged in a gap. Only the donkey got through and
ran away, the hen-perch shafts trailing on either side of
him.

Arthur and I, having come to an abrupt halt, remained
sitting in the middle of the hedge on what was left of the
vehicle, with the wheels buckling slowly beneath us. If
anyone would care to explore, I can show him where to look.
The remains may still be there. Not having the heart to
undertake a salvage operation, we walked away from the
wreckage with never a backward glance.

A Brief Dissertation on Schooling

BUSY as I was, the pursuits and activities which I have related were no more than recreational. It would seem that I lived in the manner of a playboy, idling away my time and bringing nothing in. Yet school went on, the main theme of existence. I enjoyed it on the whole and found no great difficulty with much of the curriculum. All too soon the year approached when I was to take my School Certificate Examination, which in later years was to be substituted for the General Certificate of Education — the 'O' Level — which has been given so much publicity, now itself superseded by the controversial G.C.S.E.

The rules regarding the wearing of school uniform were strictly enforced. The prefects were quick to note any irregularities in dress, such as a tie discarded or a cap in pocket when it should have been on the head, even when we were travelling to and from school on the bus. Prefects, those superior and aloof fellows, held prefects' meetings where they administered minor punishments. The major punishment was a caning by the headmaster, itself serious enough, but the ultimate measure was expulsion. Only the most reprehensible offenders were expelled, such as thieves, those who consistently ignored the rules, who persistently declined to strive for a better academic standard or who had been ill-chosen in the first place and were better out of it for their own sakes.

The new school building in which I had begun my second year was, to me, a splendid place. I was part of a very

147

reputable establishment whose fame had spread across the river into the outlying villages. The characters and incidents which I read about in 'The Magnet', could easily be adapted to my own school.

Masters swept along the long corridors, their gowns sometimes catching the floor if they had been donned hastily or carelessly. Mortar-boards were still used by one or two, as protection when making the journey from the old to the new building. The Staff, almost all graduates, were cultured men, who, when they taught us or chose to converse with us outside the classroom, expected us to understand good English fluently spoken. I, of course, was at least bi-lingual, having one language for school and my dialect for the district in which I lived.

We were an all-male society into which the opposite sex did not intrude in any way at all. Many of the masters were married, but we only saw their wives at Speech Day or Sports Day. There was never any mention of them. There were no sexual innuendos of any kind whatsoever. I never wanted my school to be anything but what it was. My views have not changed with the years. A few pupils of my own age attended Fleetwood Grammar School, which was co-educational. I never felt that I was at a disadvantage. As far as I know, for no-one had indicated otherwise, I remained normal. But 'normal' then would not necessarily mean 'normal' now.

As an adult I taught in a co-educational school for years. Although the atmosphere was agreeable enough I saw no real advantage. The sexes tended to keep themselves segregated. There were few liaisons. In saying that the boys were less boisterous and high-spirited, more restrained than in an all-boys school. I shall be accused of being, in modern parlance, male-orientated. I may well be, but on this matter I can at least speak from experience. I have known, for instance, ridiculous as it may seem, of college lecturers who have been appointed to show teachers how to teach, without ever having met the challenge of confronting a class of their own in the whole of their lives.

The standard of teaching was what one would expect of a good provincial grammar school. It ranged from excellent through good to mediocre, leaving always a few to struggle ineffectually. Much later, when as a qualified teacher I was favoured enough to be accepted as a member of the staff of a grammar school with a reputation far above the average, I found the same spread from the top downwards with two members of staff who really would have had a better life in some other career, and, more important, whose departure would have been of great profit to their unfortunate, long-suffering pupils.

The emphasis was firmly in favour of the talented and the intelligent. There was no nonsense about interpolating a lot of fringe topics. Our education was positively academic with a special emphasis laid on the 'Three R's', taken to as advanced a stage as the school could give and we could assimilate.

I was particularly fortunate in the tuition I had in English, Latin and Mathematics. I include Latin, not only because the study of it made me understand my own language better, but also because of my tutor.

Mr. Rawes, 'Bunny' Rawes to the pupils, taught English and Latin. In addition he held the post of music master, which entailed no examination work but which committed him to train a choir for the annual Speech Day, to present a concert now and again and to teach singing to the Lower School. He could not have had much time to himself for he was organist and choirmaster of St. Chad's Parish Church, Poulton-le-Fylde, which was not far from the school and from his home. As if this was not enough he was conductor of a Glee and Madrigal Society, an official of the Blackpool Musical Festival and, now I learn, a respected Freemason.

Not long after I had begun at Baines I was accepted by Mr. Rawes as a piano pupil. I said farewell to Miss Storey, who, after a last stimulating sip of tea and a final appreciation of my grandmother's sponge cake, teetered away, beladen as usual, thus closing one more early episode in life's journey.

WHEN EVERY DAY WAS SUMMER

I made my musical debut on the same platform upon which stood the staff, begowned, solemn and awesome, for morning assemblies. Now, in the big hall, used as a gymnasium during the day, the platform was a stage and there was I, immaculately turned out in full school uniform, performing a Beethoven Sonata on a grand piano, before the biggest, most sleek and prosperous-looking audience I had ever seen. It was a far cry, this sophistication and glitter, from my beach-combing outfit or my clogs and torn trousers worn at Land Hill. At another concert I joined Mr. Rawes in playing Franz Schubert's 'Marche Militaire', arranged as a duet. As Mr. Rawes was a showman as well as a performer we rattled along with tremendous elan, with suitable contrast observed for the trio.

My favourite subject and hence my forte was English Literature. So inspired was I in these lessons that I still find delight in returning to Keats, Tennyson, Chaucer and Shakespeare as well as the great novelists to which I was introduced, as an extension to those I had already met through the good offices of the Rev. Gornall.

Bunny Rawes, wiry and slightly built with the thin intelligent face of an aesthete and with wavy, greying hair straying over his collar, sat at ease before the class, for he was completely in control. Hunched in his chair, in appearance not unlike an ageing rabbit, the wise who ruled. His gown which had seen better days gathered neatly round his legs, he read long passages from 'Twelfth Night' with such obvious insight and enjoyment that for me the characters reached out of the pages. "Dost thou think, because thou art virtuous, there shall be no more cakes and ale"? quoth Sir Toby Belch to the interfering and bigotted Malvolio. I was entirely in sympathy with old Sir Toby. Why, indeed, couldn't Malvolio live and let live?

Then there was Keats' 'The Eve of St. Agnes':

"St. Agnes' Eve - Ah, bitter chill it was!
The owl, for all his feathers, was a-cold;"

All this I could visualise and agree with as a countryman,

but I marvelled at the mind which had assembled such a beautiful and balanced arrangement of words in order to capture the scene for posterity.

I would have liked to have been present in the heroine's chamber in place of young Porphyro, as gazing with bated breath he beheld that:

> *Full on the casement shone the wintry moon,*
> *and threw warm gules on Madeline's fair breast",*

What a sensitive genius had been the man who, at the end could give such pathos to the lines:

> *"And they are gone: ay, ages long ago*
> *These lovers fled away into the storm".*

And in conclusion:

> *"Angela the old*
> *Died palsy-twitch'd, with meagre face deform:*
> *The Beadsman, after thousand aves told,*
> *For aye unsought-for slept among his ashes cold".*

In English Language terms such as Subject and Predicate, Adverbial or Adjectival Clause, if not completely mastered were at least attempted and practised. We were not thrown a few blank sheets and left to our own devices to scrawl down our rambling, unco-ordinated thoughts in one long, undisciplined progression with never a comma or semi-colon, or come to that, a full stop, in sight. As opposed to 'free expression' our expression had to be controlled but not repressed, contained in selected topics, with the certainty of being reproved if we strayed. The form and shape of an essay mattered very much as did a feeling for balance and style.

History, I would have liked more if it had been about people rather than politics. Moving towards external examinations the syllabus became more and more boring for me as I was bombarded with Corn Laws and Reform Bills and a whole spate of dates which were thought to be vital, which were vital if one wanted to pass. The sense of history was there, again promoted by that paragon my grandfather, but what I was being fed was the wrong diet for me.

All these stark, dark-grey figures, being manipulated or manipulating themselves as politicians were of little if any consequence to me. I was attracted far, far more to colourful characters such as Guillem of Caberstraing who gave his heart to the lady of Castel-Roussillon, only to have that organ cut out by her husband, who had it cooked and served to his wife; or William of Poitiers, first of the early troubadours, who wrote in one of his love poems:

*"May God grant that I live long enough
to have my hands beneath her cloak".*

I found this ambition irresistible, for having arrived at puberty and an awareness of the existence of girls, I myself was not without longings in this direction, even if I was restricted within quasi-monastic confines.

Geography was one interminable succession of maps traced and coloured. These repetitive tasks were supervised by a cherubic gentleman whose ability as a teacher was barely adequate and whose class control was bordering on the non-existent. Missiles in the form of paper darts and pellets flew backwards and forwards. 'Punishment School', which meant having to stay in after school, was meted out quite prodigally, but it was only a mild deterrent to the unruly. Geography, I fear, was an outlet for high spirits which were severly curbed in most other classes. Life's texture would have been incomplete without yet another damaging blow to my personality, another punch guaranteed to deflate a confidence which was not exactly bursting at the seams. I found myself once again manoeuvred into a familiar situation, only this time it was wood, not wool.

Allotted a half-share in a bench and vice in the Woodwork Room or whatever they called this bleak chamber, the original school building, humiliated further by having to wear a sort of bibbed apron, I was prevailed upon very forcibly to make a thing to hold eggs. The prototype looked well enough I suppose, but I couldn't see what was wrong with the big white basin which stood on a slab in our pantry.

The egg-thing was rectangular with little narrow platforms at each end for it to stand on. A dozen circular holes had been bored in the top.

Accelerating the stages of construction — for even after the passage of so many years they are painful to dwell on — I succeeded in "chewing out" my dozen holes well enough with some awkward tool or other, only to find that each one was too small and would only accommodate the eggs of a thrush. At the next onslaught I misjudged and over-shot most alarmingly and was left with three or four large oval apertures which would, at a push, take goose-eggs placed on their sides. It would not work, as there were still jagged bits to be trimmed.

At the last attempt the middle, already fragile, fell in. I was left with a rickety structure with one big hole, suitable possibly for one ostrich egg. There was no demand for it in our house.

No-one raved about it. My grandfather, when it was shown to him, wore the same look of hurt disapproval as he had when I had played the B natural for the B flat. My grandmother placed my offering in the pantry it is true. There it remained neglected until it disappeared out of the house and out of existence, unworthy to be treasured even as a family memento.

Chemistry lessons and the inevitable homework left me with a tendency to break into cold tremors at the sight or mention of test-tube or pipette; a staggering bulk of formulae collected and memorised for the School Certificate Examination and forgotten immediately and forever the moment the last paper was taken in.

I managed to acquire a reasonable grasp of French as it was written, but because so little importance was given to conversation, I was very limited in speaking it when I went to France. Language laboratories were quite far in the future and there were no exchange visits between young students, at least, not for me.

Sports Day was a colourful event, reminiscent of the Edwardian summer without the straw boaters. Following the public school customs we all donned long white flannel trousers and blancoed tennis shoes, in addition to blazers, ties and caps. Somehow these additional items were provided for me. I was lucky, or rather my mother was, for Mrs. Winder, the old lady for whom she worked had a grandson older than I was, who went to Baines. Articles of uniform which he had outgrown but which were still presentable were passed on to me. Without shame or any noticeable loss of dignity I marched off to school in Tommy Winder's cast-offs. It was apparent that some garments were off-the-peg rather than made to measure, but no unkind comments were made, and they did enable me to conform to regulations.

I doubt whether any of the elite who spent much of their time in the Prefects' Common Room wore cast-offs. This cliquish, privileged 'posse' with the aloof manner and condescending attitude to those whom they considered to be small fry, offended me by their presence. They were still there, or their breed was, when I arrived in the fifth and even the sixth form. They carried favour most outrageously with those members of the staff who enjoyed and encouraged obsequious flattery. The masters concerned would understand the procedure only too well, having themselves progressed through the same system. Whether it went on at Baines to any great extent I am not in a position to judge, but there was a general tendency in public schools and therefore the grammar schools, for promising and favoured pupils to go on to university, take their degrees and return to their Alma Maters as members of staff, there to stay until death did them part. There was a continuity of scholarship and routine neither broken nor marred by external experience. In this way the Old Boys' network regenerated itself.

The prefects, whilst still in the transitional stage between boys and men, more of the former than the latter, were wont to stroll about, hands thrust deep in trouser-pockets, seemingly engaged in intense learned discourse. It was they who strolled down to the nets, be-flannelled, bats under arms, pulling on batting-gloves as they went. The click of leather on willow was their companion, especially at home or away matches on Saturday afternoons when I would be a few miles away, running wild.

When they were among us, they were ever watchful for some misdemeanour which would lead us to their presence in their own chambers. There they would indulge in sarcastic comments of a one-sided nature at our expense, knowing that it would be fool-hardy of us to strike back. Taking a leaf from their mentors' book, they selected their own favourites and those whom they hounded and derided. I managed to stay twixt and between for the most part, tolerated but not unduly oppressed. At times it was an effort to restrain myself from ruffling their plumage. A few hundred lines took time to write and I had little enough of that precious commodity for my own private pursuits.

My great failing, according to more socially-conscious was that I took everything as a joke, rules and institutions included. I was cute enough to pay lip-service to conformity. It was a great joke in itself to coast along the boundary between the orthodox and the unorthodox, sometimes slipping over when there was little danger of detection. It was a game I played, which brought me to the conclusion that life is a jest in itself, grim or macabre as it may be at times, and that there is very little that is worth worrying about for very long.

Many of us were persuaded to buy and wear enamel badges on which were engraved maps representing the League of Nations. Numerous illustrated talks were given in praise and support of this august body; collections were made to help to promote its good work. Much of the money went, of course, to maintain vast areas of conference halls and offices and to support an ever increasing body of politicians and civil servants, but there was no mention of this in the lectures. The League of Nations was at its zenith. We were assured that "peace on earth, goodwill to all men", would prevail henceforth. I was to witness its rapid decline and utter failure. Already there were ominous eruptions in

Germany. Somehow our teachers never got round to mentioning them to us. We continued on our naive course, another batch of innocents soon to be led to the slaughter.

Could I be blamed that after the War that followed, when yet another new formation called the United Nations rose up like a phoenix from the ashes, I greeted its arrival with immense scepticism and lack-lustre eyes?

Sorrow and Joy

IT was in 1935 that I passed my Grade V Examination in Pianoforte, the last one I took whilst I was with Mr. Rawes.

1935 was also the year in which my Great-uncle Tom died. His was a painful lingering death. The proximity to such sufferings in the cramped quarters of our cottage did not provide a relaxed atmosphere in which I could settle down in my final year before the School Certificate Examination.

It was said that my great-uncle had inflicted a wound on one of his toes whilst he was trying to cut his toe nails with some garden instrument which was both dirty and difficult to manipulate. Garden shears were mentioned. Though it would have been entirely in his character to try to use these in such a bizarre fashion for trimming his nails, I myself would have settled for secateurs.

Be that as it may, whatever the method he chose, the result was the same. One of his toes became infected and gangrene set in. A most offensive stench rose from his foot. The ministering angel, Mrs. Melling, was called in once more. Once more her familiar little figure was to be seen moving to and fro up the Village, along the route she had trodden three years before. My mother helped with dressings when she could, for it was my great-uncle's last wish that he should stay at home to the end. It was to her credit that she upheld his wish in spite of the discomfort it caused for everyone in the household.

The deadly malady spread to his other toes, slowly and remorselessly, until the bones were laid bare, blackened and sticking out so that their structure could be seen clearly. A tiny part of his skeleton was revealed, a part of him

157

which was already dead. I looked over my mother's shoulder and saw his swollen discoloured foot and ankle and the little black bones with their joints. I held my breath.

Though stoical to the last, as hard a man as ever lived, the intense pain overcame him at times and he would writhe about and cry out in his agony. The nights were troubled by the vocal manifestations of his desperate plight.

During his last days it was thought advisable for me to go to Land Hill. It was a 'close' night in early summer. Arthur and I were lying in bed. Outside, the roses were coming into bloom on the big bush which spread up the wall at the front of the house. Through the small window in the bedroom, to one side of the bed, a mysterious green light had appeared. Arthur and I stared at it. We sank lower under the sheets, knowing no explanation for it.

Next day my great-uncle was dead. He was buried in the double grave, lying alongside my grandfather. Two of my benefactors had now gone. It was a further sad, salutory lesson for me, also frightening in a way, that much as we are happy when things are going well, nothing lasts. From the moment we are conceived, we are borne along relentlessly on the "conveyor-belt", and there is no stopping until we are thrown off at the point selected. Some are hurled off having hardly begun, whilst others go on and on, even passing far beyond the spot when they would have liked to have left it. My great-uncle's journey on the 'belt' had been long. He had gone beyond the allotted span, healthy and content enough until the last few months. Would that his final ordeal could have been less protracted.

Thomas F. Eaves, known as 'Fred' to his contemporaries; joiner, wheelwright and undertaker, whose workshop and yard were in Out Rawcliffe, near Garstang, but who lived in Hambleton and was a pillar of the village society; Councillor of the Garstang Rural District Council; father of Annie and relative of the compassionate Mrs. Melling, submitted his bill for my great-uncle's funeral on 24th June, 1935:

	£.	s.	d.
To Oak Coffin with Solid Brass Fittings	7.	5.	0.
To New Grave and Burial Fees	1.	17.	0.
To Robe		10.	6.
To 2 Doz. Cards and Postage		7.	9.
To Obituary Notice		7.	0.
	£10.	7.	3.

The bill was paid on the same day and is receipted with two One Penny Silver Jubilee Stamps, bearing the head of King George V. (It is of interest to note that £10.00 in 1935 represented about five weeks wages for a labourer, who would be earning about £2.00 per week.)

Mr. 'Fred' Eaves, from whom my mother was soon to rent Ingol Cottage, treated her with a consideration a little above the ordinary, for they had been at school together, and were both from old-established and respected families. He had by this time taken over from his father, Mr. Thomas Eaves, who was also a notable village worthy. Years later when I was a serving soldier home on leave, I was always welcome at his house in the Village, where I had a bath, for neither Crookland Cottage, nor Ingol Cottage boasted bathrooms. It would have been inconceivable for me to depart without having a chat and a cup of tea and biscuits served by the attractive and affable Dorothy Jackson.

The venerable old gentleman, trimly-bearded, seated before a fire in his comfortable home, earned through a long life-time of endeavour and success, would tell how he, as a young man struggling to gain a foothold, had worked long, long evenings in his workshop which overlooked the Village street, situated on the left just before you go down the 'broo' to Ryecroft Corner but by this time demolished. He would see others of his age on their way to the pub and would console himself with the fact that whilst he was earning sixpence they would be spending the same, so he would be a shilling better off. His sagacious advice did not fall upon deaf ears. When I was in a similar position, striving to earn a little extra and working from my own home in the evenings, seeing other folk sauntering up the road for a drink, I paid silent homage to Mr. Eaves. I liked, respected and admired him. He died whilst I was home on one of my leaves and I made a special point of attending his funeral.

1935 had something else momentous to offer. My Uncle Ben, who had put in brief appearances throughout my childhood and adolescence had been courting a young woman for some time. She was a farmer's daughter who came from Out Rawcliffe. During the evenings when she and my Uncle Ben had finished work (she was employed as help to a farmer's wife and 'lived in') they would pay occasional visits. If my Great-uncle Tom was present it caused even more embarrassment than normal, for he had taken an instant dislike to Uncle Ben's intended partner. She did nothing to ingratiate herself with him as she talked constantly and loudly. My great-uncle would mutter imprecations, audible enough for all to hear, whenever she appeared.

Uncle Ben's young lady had very orthodox views about young folk going out to work earlier rather than later. Or was it a case of what was good enough for her was good enough for others, which meant me? Or was it because she was afraid that Uncle Ben might have to contribute to his mother's upkeep should anything befall my mother? With nuptials already being planned there would be barely enough to manage on as it was. For whatever reason, she was not above "putting the boot in", with increasing frequency.

One morning in August the unprecedented happened. Consternation reigned. My Uncle Ben and his young lady had up and got married without any prior warning. The union had been blessed in Hambleton Church, just up the road. Only the best man and bridesmaid had witnessed the ceremony.

My grandmother's only son, in whom she was well pleased, my mother's only brother in whom, at times, she was not so well pleased, had actually undertaken such an event, second only to a funeral in their social calendar, without inviting them to be present, without even telling them about it. It was tantamount to a criminal act.

As if conveyed at the speed of light the fateful news was sprung on the infallible village grapevine, which acted just as quickly as divine communication. As if it were not enough to discover that only a token force had been representative at the wedding, it was now found that the wayward and secretive couple, intent on escaping as quickly as possible the wrath that would surely come, had sped with all due speed to the Isle of Man. It was a classic example of "live now, pay later". In their fervent desire to place an expanse of water betweem themselves and irate relatives left stamping their feet on the mainland, they were re-enacting the flights of countless renegade lovers who had preceded them.

Secretly I hoped that it would turn out to have been a "shotgun marriage". I watched and listened but was disappointed for it was evident this was not the case. Of course, there was no hint of such a mischievous suspicion from my grandmother or my mother, for whom all sexual matters, however mild, were taboo.

Recriminations abounded when the couple, confirmed in their love, returned from foreign parts. Exchanges smouldered on, fanned into conflagrations by my mother who was always loathe to let affronts, real or imagined, peter out. As they did not concern me, I steered well clear.

Whilst mentioning the Isle-of-Man one of my Uncle Ben's acquaintances from his threshing-days had confided in him that he would not undertake the short trip from mainland to island by air, as he had been told that the Irish Sea was infested with sharks. Should there be an accident he didn't relish meeting his end by being eaten. On further deliberation, however, he had decided that it would be marginally less painful than being devoured slowly by an old sow. It was a well known fact that if you were unwise enough to lie down in a pigsty occupied by this animal you would be tempting providence.

The Demon Intrudes

UNAWARE of it as I was at the time subtle changes were taking place in my outlook, forces previously subdued were now coming out into the open. As I grew in stature (by the time I was sixteen I had reached my full height of nearly six feet), and reached out towards manhood, my mental outlook altered or was forced to alter, not overnight but insidiously. A restlessness which besets birds before they migrate, or an instinct which impels fledglings to fly, to become independent of parents, was invading my system.

I had a responsibility, one which I could have done without, to do as well as I could at school in order to go on and do even better by finding a job which "befitted my education". The term was my mother's, not mine. She was overcome with desire for me to 'better myself', by going to work in a suit and collar and tie, rather than overalls and heavy boots (clogs were on the way out). Without in the least disparaging my mother, I have since wondered whether it was not only for my sake that she persisted. Was it also a subconscious urge that through my success she would redeem some of that dignity and pride which had been so badly damaged when I was born?

In spite of the enlightenment I had received beyond the "perimeter fence", the academic and artistic qualities in me, which later flowered and bore fruit, were barely beyond the seedling state. I would have been content enough, I had thought, to have spent my life in the open air, toiling in the fields as my forebears had done. My mother was in a position to look both ways, not liking what she saw in the past. She was only too well aware that my grandfather had been entrapped, tending the land as a menial, having to

163

take orders instead of giving them. Her brother was in a similar position to most of his ancestors. Here was an opportunity for someone to escape at last. I couldn't see it, but she could.

Not entirely without a conscience, and possessing some sensitivity, I tried to conform to her wishes. Would that I could have been forced into a retreat for a year or two. As it was, the fields and the woods remained, as did the River (but not so much now), as did Land Hill. I was not strong enough to reject enticement. The tasks of study and revision which I set myself were often left incomplete. For me, at this time, before I came to learn what discipline really meant, the 'Gates of Hell' were paved with good intentions.

I cannot say that tremendous incentives were dangled before my eyes, glittering and attractive. As I have said, as far as I knew then, with no financial means available, a university place was unattainable. To be articled to a solicitor meant putting down a considerable sum of money, which was quite out of the question. There would have been ways, there always are if one is tenacious enough, but I was entirely ignorant as to the means of achieving them.

Hints were beginning to arise, aimed in my direction which grew into more than hints. Was it not time that a big lad like me was at work, bringing some money in?

My mother stuck rigidly to her aim. She was in the minority in being unselfish and enlightened enough to reject the old idea that a child was to start earning, to bring money in as soon as possible, regardless of his potential. We were not in such desperate circumstances, it appeared, at least according to my mother, to take such a drastic decision.

I was pulled in at least two ways if not more. There was external pressure for me to leave school, stronger internal pressure that I should not. I could hardly be unaware that the majority of my age group were already working, either as farm labourers or apprentices in trades, and had been for a couple of years. Granted, they did not take much home in those early years and those on farms would not earn a great deal even when they came of age. The comparison was there, nevertheless.

Because of inner conflicts which resulted from all the uncertainty and insecurity, it is surprising that I managed to retain any confidence at all. My poor confidence was for most of the time too diffident to show itself in this disturbed environment, biding its time until its owner was to move eventually to one which better suited it.

The period between sixteen and eighteen was not a happy one on the whole. Storm clouds gathered overhead with only short interludes of warmth and sunlight between. Each one was followed by an inevitable return to grey skies.

It was during this troubled period, that I began to realise that I would never remain in the village. Had I inherited a restlessness of spirit from my father who had been possessed by a wild, roving demon when he was young? This paternal figure, with none of a father's power, turned up now and again, quite unsolicited, for he still professed to be attracted to my mother although he was married with a family of his own. She rejected this continued interest for propriety's sake if for nothing else. People talked in a village and our village would have won first prize had there been an award for gossiping. I had a sneaking feeling, though she would strongly oppose my suggestion of it, that there was still affection left for him. If physical qualities had anything to do with it, there were good reasons why women would find him appealing. Tall and well built, he carried himself well. There was a certain devilish handsomeness about him. He gave me the impression that he was afraid of nothing. Always, on the brief occasions when I saw him he wore a navy blue suit with collar and tie. Old soldier that he was, the toe-caps of his boots or shoes were like mirrors and his turn-out was as for a ceremonial parade. If he had been responsible for a dastardly deed on my mother's person, as was whispered by some, it would have been a bold and foolhardy person who would have said it to his face. Being half-Irish he had a volatile temper and was quick to respond to affronts.

Was it that history was repeating itself in this new urge, still only faintly stirring; was it a desire to run away and escape from irritating problems or was it a natural cry from the primeval past for the young man to spread wings and take flight? Probably it was a mixture of all these. A psychiatrist would be able to throw some light, but I am not all that interested. All I know is that it happened. I was comfortable and well cared for at home — in all respects better than most. Only a fool would even consider leaving the comfort of a feather-bed to exchange it for a ground sheet on sodden ground in some foreign field. Yet eventually this was the voluntary course which I took.

The books I turned to for recreational reading helped to fan my longing to travel far, far beyond the flat expanse of the Fylde. I read the 'Sanders of the River' series by Edgar Wallace and saw myself as a young district commissioner in some far-flung outpost of Empire. We could still boast that the sun never set on our mighty British Empire. Few people were misguided enough to sneer at patriotism. So there I was, alone in the jungle, dressed for dinner with my native servants in attendance, with the drums throbbing out their message in the distance. My romanticised concept took no account of irritating insects, oppressive heat, discomfort, disease and loneliness.

After I had read F. Yeats Brown's 'Bengal Lancer' I looked up from my school books more and more often, away beyond the classroom window, to India and the North West Frontier where in the heat-haze battles were being fought between the hawk-eyed tribesmen and the troops of the British Raj. I wasn't to know it, but soon I would be meeting some of the men who were already soldiering there whilst I still sat at my desk. I doodled away in my rough-book, drawing military figures in K.D. shorts and pith helmets. I bored my colleagues at school with constant reference to military topics to such an extent that they called me 'The Brigadier'. The seeds were sown. Looking back, I see now

that it was inevitable that when I was old enough to take
'The King's Shilling' I would be off.

In the summer of 1936 I took my School Certificate
Examination. The results, predictably, were not as good as
they might have been for the multiplicity of reasons already
put forward. I gained a 'good' mark in English, reached
'credit' standard in History, Geography and French, and
'pass' marks in Latin and Mathematics.

My success in Geography must have been due to Mr.
Moulding, an alert and vigorous young master who was
known, sub voce, by the curious pseudonym of 'Piggy',
though he resembled this animal neither in appearance nor
in manners.

With one more credit I should have gained Matriculation
Exemption, thereby qualifying me for entry to a university.
I had Latin and Mathematics which were obligatory subjects. It was decided that I should convert one of the passes
into a credit during the following year, my first year in the
sixth form.

The sixth form in those days was very small, most by now
having diverted themselves into employment. In the first
year sixth at the beginning of the autumn term in 1936
there could not have been more than a dozen students, if
that. After consultation I elected to study English Literature, History and French. Under more favourable circumstances at home, I would have been only too happy to
do so, and was for a time. The curriculum had been nar-
rowed down to my favourite subjects and I enjoyed what I
was doing.

I became more and more self-conscious, guilt-ridden and
ill-at-ease. I suppose it was I who really persuaded, even
forced my mother to accept that I should, after all, seek
employment. I left Baines in the summer of 1937, after one
year in the sixth form.

Mr. F.J. Stafford, M.A., M.Ed., the Headmaster, said this
in his final paragraph of my reference:

> *"Bowman is a boy of excellent character. He is*
> *steady, hard-working, and most reliable. His mother*

has made great sacrifices in order to give the boy a
good education and he, on his part, has spared no
pains to profit from the opportunity thus provided.
He is intelligent, neat in appearance and
well-mannered. I have no doubt that he would render
good service".

I cannot help feeling that the headmaster was perhaps too generous in his appraisal, but I am still proud to have it. For Mr. Stafford I had the highest regard. He ruled quietly and efficiently, was one of the 'old school' of headmasters. Scrupulously fair, it was obvious that he was respected by staff and pupils alike. He it was who greeted me back to the school after the War, when I took my young wife on a visit; he it was who found time to sit down with us and give me some sound advice as to which way I should plan my future career.

The Rev. Gornall's final reference struck more below the surface and was, as I read it, a veiled rebuke. But then, it was he who had been horrified to see me ride a cow in calf; had been appalled to hear dance music pealing forth from his consecrated pile. To Mr. Stafford these manifestations of crass unruliness had never been revealed.

The Rev. Gornall wrote as follows:

"He was a Scholar at the Council School,
Hambleton, before going to Baines Grammar School.
He has great possibilities if he will use his gifts, for
undoubtedly he has the ability to achieve great
things. He belongs to an old respected family in this
neighbourhood and his character is all you would
require".

I thought the bit about character was ambiguous, open-ended, the sort of statement that could mean all things to all men.

Between my Uncle Ben's marriage and leaving school my grandmother, my mother and I had moved to Ingol Cottage, about a hundred yards nearer the Village from our old cottage. This new abode of ours lay bck off the village street at a small 'T' junction. It was of the 'two-up two-down' type, with a low pantry attached at the back. The stone sink, or

A view of 'the Village', showing the gable-end of Ingol Cottage in the centre.

'slop-stone', was in the kitchen. There was still no bath or hot water.

Outside, close to the back door was a sturdy brick wash-house. On the other side of the house was a wooden lean-to in which a good stock of coal was kept for our open fires. At the back was quite a sizeable garden-cum-orchard on a level considerably higher than the house. A cindered path led to a small building of such familiar design that its purpose needed no explanation. To reach this necessary house, further away and more exposed than at Crooklands Cottage, one had to pass a pigsty which was next to it.

We settled into our new home comfortably enough. It was luxury indeed to have a separate parlour, sitting-room or front room, with my piano in it, and easy chairs and the sofa. Soon when I was working full-time on a farm, I would gain great comfort and pleasure from lying on the sofa, reading in front of a good fire. The warmth would close round me, physically tired as I was after carting manure or spreading it, not with mechanical means but with a muck-fork. The wind to which I had been exposed all day would still howl in the chimney. Here it could not reach me.

'Let Joy Be Unconfined'

IN 1938 and on to 1939 Margaret of Land Hill, a great one for dances, light as thistle-down, had taught me to dance. Both Arthur and I were quite adept at dances then in vogue. There was the Fox-trot, Waltz, Veleta, Military Two-step, Barn Dance and Polka and a new one called the Palais Glide. The Charleston enjoyed a brief popularity. We young ones occasionally had a crack at the Lancers, though this was somewhat specialised, a treasured heirloom of a previous age. I must confess that I was never much good at the Slow Fox-trot which I thought was for show-offs and those sinuous males with oily, sneaky natures.

Margaret, fount of insatiable energy, organised and produced concert parties. Her base was Hambleton Reading Room where Tom was on the committee and for years its chairman. Her ambition did not stop at Hambleton for she took us on tour to the neighbouring villages. Of course, Arthur and I were integral members of a cast which performed sketches, songs, dances and musical extravaganzas in the form of revues. It was all great fun and we drew packed audiences.

Then there was the band. I have forgotten when it was actually formed, but for me it extended over a year or two up to 1939, when I left it. History was indeed repeating itself. Not now my Great-uncle Dick with his violin or piccolo, my grandfather with his cello, but Arthur and I who replaced them, playing on the self-same stage in a room virtually unchanged down to the decor, now faded and in places, peeling. Revellers rejoicing at the 'Relief of Mafeking' would have still felt at home.

Arthur played the drums, or rather the percussion, and I played the piano. There was a blind gentleman on the violin and Jimmy Bleasdale, a contemporary of ours, on the saxophone. Following the fashion of the big bands we donned white shirts, winged collars and bow-ties. We followed avidly the progress of the conductors and leading soloists in these great dance bands. When Harry Roy brought his famous band to Blackpool we were wildly enthusiastic about it and made a special journey to be present. The 'Melody Maker' was compulsive reading. I suppose that were I eighteen again, I would be part of a group, surrounded by flashing lights and guitars and hammering out 'pop' music for all I was worth on an electrically-operated keyboard.

Orders increased. We travelled far and wide to Out Rawcliffe, Pilling and beyond, not on foot as in previous ages, but by motor car or van. For the first time in my life I had some money of my own. With the energetic residents congregated from the whole district revolving below us (for folk travelled quite long distances to a 'stir' or 'stor' as it was called, often on bicycles in the most inclement weather), we played the nights away and into the early mornings.

> *"Toodle Luma Luma, Toodle Luma Luma, Toodle Aye a*
> *Any umbrellas, any umbrellas to fix today"*

sang the dulcet tones of Jimmy's saxophone. Young lovers drew closer. Assignations were arranged. Carefree for the moment, lulled by the smooth cooing, turtle-dove sound of the melodies of the late 1930s the dancers went round and round, hypnotised by the constant circular movement, jointly performed. Unwittingly they danced, for they were unaware for the most part, or indifferent to the baying of the mastiffs or to the mad Walpurgis dance then escalating in Germany.

They were dancing themselves into a dark age in which

insecurity and violence would dominate. Never again would it be the same. Just as the young ones in my grandfather's time had danced to different tunes, unmindful of the dreadful fate which awaited many of them, so it was now.

Came the dawn, for Arthur and me it was a different story. Poor sleepy Arthur, stumbling out of the back door of his farmhouse, into the unwelcoming darkness with his storm-lamp shedding only a faint light, made his way towards the shippon, clutching milking-can and stool. I slightly more awake for I had travelled from home, either walking or on bicycle.

* * * *

During this period I applied for various 'collar-and-tie' posts, going through the ritual of reproducing my references in long-hand. For my first interview, I put on my navy blue suit with a matching shirt and tie and cycled to Knott-End, where a V.I.P. lived. With immense solemnity a maid ushered me into the great man's presence. I knew she was a maid because she was dressed like one. She had a condescending aloof manner which went with the house.

Splendour encompassed this gentleman. Here was wealth and security, the peak of human endeavours. What I did not know was that here, as in many such places, there was the likelihood of oppression. He leant against his great mahogany table and assessed me with eyes which I can only describe as porcine. I had seen these eyes watching my every move, from sties where their owners waited to be fed, and had known that if I should have been so misguided as to have lain down, those swine would have eaten me.

As the owner of these eyes was very short and fat, with a great red neck bulging way over his collar, it was not surprising that he showed a symptom of being grossly unfit. Even when stationary he was very short of breath. I could not take to this man; nor did I try very much; nor did I think that he had warmed to me. I stood well above him in stature, was very lean and fit and above all, was young;

whilst he, for all his local eminence was none of these things.

I have no idea what was said. His patronage and condescension far out-reached those of his maid, and could not have drawn out the best in me. I may have retaliated, probably did, in a way which the Army would call dumb insolence. My humble origins were forgotten, the servility which should have come to my rescue was nowhere to be seen. I was not openly rude as I was conditioned successfully to be good-mannered. Nevertheless, it was obvious when we parted that I was not the man for him. I was never summoned to the County Offices and thus escaped a fate worse than death.

Whatever it was, perhaps divine intervention or a chance encounter, I was freed from a cage which would have been most restrictive. Instead of becoming a 'battery-bird' I was given the privilege of becoming a 'free-range fowl'. But not before a further attempt had been made to snare me.

Why, oh why did I apply for and be accepted by of all people, a photographer. I had never had the slightest interest in a camera, never knew how one worked, never wanted to. Yet there I was storing my bicycle in a photographer's shop in a back street near Central Station, Blackpool, all ready for the day's work. Faded prints of weddings and family groups were on display, faintly seen through the grimy plate-glass window. It was by no means a high class establishment in which I was to start my career. But one never knew. Look at 'David Copperfield'. The narrow cobbled street stank strongly of urine, for it was here that holiday visitors emptied their bladders after 'heavy' drinking in the sleazy pubs round Central Station.

My apprenticeship or training in this insalubrious place did not last long. Maybe I did not give it a fair chance, for I was only there two days. It seemed like a millenium. Decades were spent with my overseer in a little room with no lights. Here in the darkness I watched, with no enthusiasm

at all, as unknown people's faces emerged from the nega-
tives which were placed in shallow trays and washed about.

I felt like the condemned man in Oscar Wilde's 'The
Ballad of Reading Gaol' who looked

"with such a wistful eye
Upon that little tent of blue
Which prisoners call the sky".

Presumably, when he was not taking exercise he had a
window in his cell. I had none.

My boss, the seedy little man with the duplicity and
obsequiousness of 'Uriah Heep', with the greasy hair and
the unpleasant body odour, would reach for his stained and
belted raincoat and we would venture forth on expeditions.
Draped all about in curiously-shaped boxes and weighed
down with miniature sets of scaffolding, our first visit took
us to an hotel at South Shore, to record for posterity a large
assembly of raddled harridans and their aged, repulsive
escorts. I could not imagine why they should want such a
memento. Had I looked like any one of them I should have
been only too happy to be excluded. I tried in vain to
assemble a tripod out of the scaffolding and failed. Stung by
the muttered criticisms of my manipulator I stood in the
background receding further and further, whilst he
crouched under the cover of his camera. I wished that I was
an explosives expert, so that he would blow himself up
when he pulled his cord or whatever it was that he had to
operate. I would also like to have caused dreadful havoc
among that lot there who were pointed their imbecile grins
camera-wards. Surely they were not real people. None of it
was real. It was all a nightmare. Holiday-makers, tripod,
ridiculous equipment.

The next day, it must have been the next day for I only
lasted for two, we went to a bowling green where there was
a presentation. There were more ridiculous poses with a big
gleaming cup in the middle. Officious men in bowler hats
and extended waistcoats on which sat watch-chains formed
this assembly. They were just as bad.

When we returned to the studios I informed my boss that

I was going home and would not be returning. It was with mutual relief that we parted; with lasting relief that we never saw each other again. I wheeled out my Raleigh Roadster, pointed it towards Hambleton and trod on the pedals for all I was worth. My mother sniffed at my lack of tenacity. No moral fibre. I was turning out to be a bit of a drifter.

The Formidable Critchleys

THE two or three months from August to the end of
October or early November of 1937 turned out to be
so memorable and enjoyable that every time I think
of this period it is with pleasure and gratitude.

I was in a 'stop-gap' job, understood from the outset to be
only very temporary. I earned very little and had to work
hard for what I got. Yet during those few weeks in late
summer and into autumn I cycled to work every morning
with a light heart, eager to join my work-mates.

My Uncle Ben, who was now employed by Mr. George
Critchley of Crane Hall Farm, Out Rawcliffe, lived in a
rented cottage very near to Rawcliffe Hall. Crane Hall
Farm, once the home farm, was adjacent to the Hall.

Both Hall and Farm were near to the River Wyre, now
much narrower and a few miles nearer to its source than it
was at Hambleton. About half a mile away was Cartford
Bridge, a narrow toll bridge joining Out Rawcliffe to Great
Eccleston.

My Uncle Ben approached Mr. Critchley about taking me
on as an extra hand for the harvest. Mr. Critchley had a
large farm to run and several mouths to feed. Astute and
enterprising, he foresaw that he must keep abreast of new
trends in this lean period for farmers or he would be in
danger of joining those who were running close to bank-
ruptcy. As he had chosen not to stand still but to introduce
new schemes, he must have had considerable additional
overheads to meet.

Why did Mr. Critchley allow me to join his workforce for

a while? Although I was fit and able to tackle most jobs on a farm, compared to Mr. Critchley and his men I was a mere inexperienced "strip of a lad". For those extra three years at school, others of my age had gained three years experience on the land. Was it sympathy for my present plight, a small aberration in better judgement, which prompted Mr. Critchley's decision, in which I suspect Mrs. Critchley had a hand? Or was it Christian charity? Mrs. Critchley was not only a staunch believer but she practised what she believed, which in my experience is very rare indeed. The slip of a lad was privileged to be admitted to the household and soon treated as one of their own. Privileged to work the long golden days in company in which there was no back-biting, in which helpfulness and kindliness prevailed. It all seems too good to be true, but for that brief spell, that was how it was.

Mr. and Mrs. Critchley had a family of three sons and two daughters. The two girls, Gwen and Jean, were very pretty and were both, I think, younger than I. What struck me most of all was the size of the male members of the family. Father would be described as "stiff-built", but to me he seemed immense. Two of the sons, Thomas and Ronnie, were built like their father. Thomas was my senior by a few years, but Ronnie was a year or two my junior and was still growing and developing. Nevertheless, at his age he could raise two 56lb. weights above his head, one in each hand and bang them together. Half-hundredweight bags were thrown carelessly on one side to make room for hundredweights, also thrown about with nonchalant ease.

All three were interested and skilled in Cumberland wrestling. Most young males on farms, whether employers or employees had an inclination towards this sport. Dependant upon strength as well as skill, it was yet another manifestation of male supremacy, a display of physical power, not without arrogance and comparable to that shown by rutting stags. The strain of body grappling against body, the side-stepping, the great snorts and grunts were all there. All that was missing were the locked antlers.

The Critchleys being very powerful, thick-set and short-ish in stature were constructed to withstand desperate attempts to upset their balance. Their feet, locked to the ground by great, taut thigh-muscles, held fast against efforts to dislodge them.

How then did I, slender and untutored as I was, survive my sojourn with these giants? The truth is they never laid hands on me in anger, never made the slightest attempt to belittle me, either physically or with jibes at my short-comings. I was very fortunate. On other farms that I could mention it would have been vastly different and life for me would have been made very uncomfortable. With the Critchleys it was not so. If Thomas showed me a 'cross-but-tock' — one of the throws in the style of wrestling which he practised — it was a demonstration rather than a show of superior strength, for he could have hurled me about and crippled me had he felt so inclined. My bouts with Ronnie were either instructive or playful, for had he been mali-cious, which he certainly was not, he also could have "had me for breakfast".

In addition to my Uncle Ben, two other men were em-ployed by Mr. Critchley. Both were as yet unmarried. One was Mr. Bill Mason who 'lived in'. His birthplace, if I remember correctly, was in that wild area which lies to the north of Lancaster. I never discovered why Mr. Mason was known as 'Wind', but everyone called him that. In appear-ance he reminded me of one of the Geography masters at Baines, but was a very much younger, slimmer fitter ver-sion. Wind had a cherubic face of the kind which smiles down benignly from ledges in mediaeval churches. He was a listener rather than a talker; a silent assessor not given to forcing his own beliefs on others. A few words went a long way with Wind. But when witty remarks appropriate to our own region were flying about in the dialect, he could throw in a few apt ones of his own, quietly delivered, and laugh as heartily as the rest of us.

The other member of Mr. Critchley's staff, certainly not

least in importance, was Mr. Bill Butler, the horseman. He lived not far from Uncle Ben, just round the corner from the farm. Bill was known as 'Stout-un'. This meant 'the stout one', or one who carried a lot of weight physically. He had inherited this nickname from his father, so Bill was really 'Young Stout-un'. If ever there was a misnomer here was one, for he was as lean as a wolf. I learnt from my Uncle Ben that 'Old Stout-un', the original, had received his name, which was ironically given, whilst he was still at school, because he was so inordinately thin. Bill had an aquiline face, on which his nose was a prominent feature. Though not of the same shape as my great-uncle's, it had a similar rosy hue but no 'nodules'.

Like all the others at Crane Hall, Bill went out of his way to guide me. I could so easily have been the butt of his jokes, a ready target for his piercing wit, but no such baiting ever occurred. He was a great character, for whom I formed a liking and respect.

No wonder Bill was thin. In addition to this paternal inheritance he would plough an acre a day during certain months of the year. In so doing he would walk upwards of twelve miles behind his two great horses and his plough, Ploughing was a specialist's job. Watchful and critical eyes were always observing the ploughman's work. The merits or shortcomings of specific ploughmen were discussed in pubs. If there was a 'kink' in the furrows as seen from the road, derision and scorn would be poured on the ploughman whose eye wasn't as straight as it should have been. Bill was considered to be an expert, one of the very best.

His legs were long and very thin. The thinness was accentuated by the knee-breeches and the leggings which he wore. They were cylindrical from ankle to knee and covered lower limbs which my grandmother would have described as 'pipe-stoppers' or 'pipe-cleaners'. Some years later in North Africa I saw the uncovered version and was reminded instantly of Bill Butler. Bill was only too aware of his lean shanks. He turned the joke on himself by reminding everyone fairly constantly that his "calves were out at grass". This play upon the word 'calves' meant that they were not in evidence because they had been put out to pasture. The fact that he did not have great, bulging calf muscles did not hinder him from walking mile after mile in the long straight furrows made by his plough, "one foot up, one foot down" as he put it.

In the warm stable, after his charges the big Shires had been rubbed down, fed and bedded down for the night, and were chomping and stamping their great feet before they settled, Stout-un would sit on an upturned bucket or a bag of chaff, and with his 'fag' dangling from one corner of his mouth as he talked, would tell us of his exploits, possibly extended and embroidered for my greater entertainment. His eyes twinkled as he delivered examples of his dry humour. For me it was one laugh after another. Contemplating Bill's waggish nature, I am sure it must have been he who christened 'Wind', just as he christened Thomas 'Prince', and young Ronnie 'Scroggins'. I never knew what name he decided for me, but there would be one, and it would be very suitable.

Ale was never far from his mind nor his conversation. He was a frequent customer at the Cartford Inn, then a small hostelry just over Cartford Bridge, where ale was still served straight from the wood. Ploughing, carting, mowing, harvesting were all thirsty work. The mirage of a pint glass with a good 'collar' on it must have led Bill onwards over many a weary mile. The donkey had his carrot, the workman his few jars of beer. Saturday nights were anticipated throughout the week from Monday morning onwards.

The attractions of agricultural shows were not only related to animals and machinery. Most farm workers were allowed a few hours off to visit these rural events. After a perfunctory inspection of the pens and the flower tents, some made a beeline for the beer tent or the pubs, which were more than likely to have a licence to stay open all day. It was at Great Eccleston show that one of Stout-un's acquaintances had "taken aboard a greater load than he could carry". In the evening, not being able to ride his bicycle, he had attempted to wheel it homewards.

Somewhere near to Cartford Bridge, this character had decided to give up the battle and to take a rest by the wayside. This he did. When he awoke it was with growing consternation that he found he was clad only in his 'combinations', those quaint looking woollen garments in which long-sleeved buttoned vests and long underpants are joined together. The vision of this unfortunate, pedalling home in the dawn, bereft of all except his small-clothes and feeling very poorly, must have caused early risers coming from the opposite direction to run off the road at this apparition. He was lucky in that there would be very few using his route at that time of the morning.

Stout-un himself had been the hero of a similar adventure at Great Eccleston, at the Silver Jubilee celebrations for King George V. As usual he was in 'his cups' by nightfall, but had gallantly elected to see a lady friend home. A veil is drawn on what went on exactly in that turbulent night, not to save the lady's feelings, but because Bill, when he woke up in a field in the morning, could not remember anything at all of what had taken place.

Being on foot, he started to walk homewards. It went without saying that he also would be feeling 'very poorly'. He travelled some distance before he became aware that his legs were cold. On looking down it was to his surprise that he found that he was minus his trousers, or, as he would say, his 'breeches'. His legs were not entirely bare, however, for he was still clad in his long flannel underwear, an essential part of his dress in all weathers. Even in high summer, with perspiration running all over the place, Stout-un never discarded these garments. Did he retrace his flagging steps to retrieve his breeches? I forget.

When I arrived for work Bill would be coming down the yard, or 'gearing up' in the stable.

It was a big stable with seven stalls. There were usually up to five working horses in it, the majority being Shires with one or two Clydesdales. After greeting each other (he usually called me "young man"), I enquired after his health. More often than not he would reply that he was very poorly, which indicated that he had had a 'heavy session' on the previous evening.

It was understood that I should have all my meals at the farm. Had I stayed at Crane Hall for a year I would have filled-out and come nearer to matching the stockiness of Thomas and Ronnie and Bill Mason. Within a couple of years I might even have become a wrestling partner for Thomas himself. Who knows?

The kitchen at Crane Hall was spacious, high-ceilinged and rectangular. I have the impression that it was light, airy and sparsely furnished. Down the centre ran a long wide table of bare wood. When this table was empty it was scrubbed clean, as was everything else that was scrubbable in Mrs. Critchley's home.

At meal times the table was laid for all the menfolk, though I think that at times Mrs. Critchley joined us. For special occasions such as threshing days extra places would be laid, but there was still room to spare round that great table.

It was soon discovered that I had a voracious appetite. Bill Butler, the alert and observant one, had probably been the first to notice how quickly I had gobbled my porridge with the sugar and fresh milk added. "Give 'im some side-boards, Missis", Bill had said, "side-boards is what 'e needs on 'is dish".

Side-boards, it may be recalled, were those structures which were fitted to farm-carts at certain times in order to increase the volume of the load. There was absolutely no resentment at my greediness. A laugh had gone round the table. The 'Old Man' had sealed it with his approval by laughing with the rest. My 'side-boards' became a standing joke. Next morning and on all other mornings my dish was bigger and wider and deeper than the rest.

Oh, that porridge. I thought about it when I went to bed and again as I pedalled through Town End and along Wyre-side in those cool early mornings, with a heavy dew lying everywhere. Mrs. Critchley, that neat, matronly lady, outwardly displaying a well-bred reserve but inwardly so warm-hearted, is remembered by me for many kindnesses, but most of all for the breakfast porridge and the 'side-boards'.

Of course, breakfast did not stop at that. There followed traditional fare, lots of it with home-made bread and fresh butter unlimited and mugs of tea. I reeled out of that kitchen puffing like an old man and unbelievable as it seems now, went straight into the fields to perform some energetic task which entailed a lot of bending.

As my Uncle Ben often said, and he had sampled the good and the bad, "Crane Hall was a good place for meat". This was an understatement.

The suppers laid on at harvest time were extravaganzas. In September when the weather was favourable, as it was in the year 1937, work went on from as soon as the sun had dried the dew until late at night. When the harvest moon was rising, carts could still be heard trundling along the tracks in the silent evening; figures could still be seen in silhouette setting up the corn or throwing up the sheaves on to carts and lorries. when the light went altogether or when the boss decided to call it a day we trooped up the yard and into the kitchen to attack the spread which was set out ready for us. That great table must have had some solid legs, for every inch of it was covered with good, plain food, which suited me down to the ground. Fresh bread and butter, slices of cheese cut from an enormous piece, cold ham, tomatoes, apple pie, cake — it was all there.

Did I read somewhere that a person of breeding should always leave a little on the plate in appreciation of the hostess's cuisine or something to that effect? Was it one of the rules of etiquette, like sticking the little finger out when holding a cup? My grandfather was fond of saying that it was good for people to leave the table still "unfulfilled".

I subscribed to neither of these refinements. Not one crumb remained on my plate; nor was I able to eat another morsel when I left the table.

Alongside The Men

"FAIR waved the golden corn". The cornfields in the Fylde, mainly wheat and oats, had turned from green to yellow in the preceding months of July and August and were now ready for harvesting. After we had 'opened up' a field with scythes to prepare a clear space round the gate, Bill Butler drove in the self-binder and began to cut wide swathes, going round and round and working inwards all the while.

The agricultural machine was called a self-binder because not only did it cut the corn but it also collected the stalks into sheaves and bound them. Less advanced or more pecunious farmers still used the reaping machine which just cut the crop. Labourers followed the path of the machine, making their own sheaves and tying them with bands of twisted strands of straw.

We, with our advanced technology, with half the work done for us, set the sheaves up by leaning them upright and together in groups of eight to form hut-like structures. Each farmer had his own idea on the formation. A couple more sheaves might be placed on top, for instance, as a 'hood'. Each batch was called an 'attock'. When the wind and sun had dried them, they were ready for loading and carting.

The fields in this region, though bearing no comparison to those in counties like Lincolnshire, were still generally bigger than those round Hambleton. By the end of a long day which did not finish at five o'clock, but which might go on for another five or six hours, one realised that there were quite a few attocks in a twenty-acre field.

Just as the hay had been reached on to carts and lorries, so were the sheaves tossed upwards. As with everything else there was a 'knack' in flicking the sheaf off the twin

184

prongs of the pitch fork. The corn was usually stacked in the stack-yard where it would be handy for the thresher. If the stacks were not destined to be threshed fairly soon, they would have to be thatched to keep the contents dry. This thatching process, called 'thacking' in the dialect, was a skilled job, one in which my grandfather had excelled.

Threshing days were hard. The thresher men were itine-rants, in a sense nomads, for they ranged far and wide over the countryside, at the beck and call of the boss who or-ganised their itinerary. Theirs was a varied diet in quality and quantity. They rarely ate at the same farm twice during a season. When they sat down they were always in a hurry. This proud, restless breed seemed to revel in dust, dirt and grease. At nightfall they would be seen, lone solitary figures, wending their way homeward on bicycles to roost. As they passed by, still energetic enough to shout a hearty greeting, their eyes and teeth gleamed in contrast against their dusky faces, still unwashed.

My Uncle Ben followed a thresher during the Second World War. Though he complained about the unsocial hours and the unceasing labour, I think he secretly enjoyed the life. It pandered to his independent spirit. He was certainly not chained to one spot, nor was he governed too much by the clock. On an audience which changed con-stantly he was able to practise his gift as a raconteur (which, like that of Stout-un was not inconsiderable), with less danger of causing yawns of boredom. Most important of all, he got more money than he would have done on a farm.

The anecdotes which my Uncle Ben collected during his threshing days are legion. I interpolate a couple of these, which are about food, in order to indicate that queasy stomachs were not for thresher-men.

On the table was a jar. By its colour and texture its contents were either blackberry or blackcurrant jam. When my Uncle Ben fancied a taste and reached for the jar, the berries or currants took wing and flew away. It was only then that they were recognised as a swarm of flies which

My Uncle Ben, still with a good tale to tell, in 1987.

had congregated in the pot. Another time my uncle was hastily devouring his first course when he heard a 'clop-clopping' sound over by the fireplace in the farm kitchen. Looking sideways he saw that the dog was lapping up rice pudding from a large, blackened pan which had been placed on the hearth in readiness for serving. The lady of the house, hovering near, clad in an apron bright with grease, delivered a mild admonishment to the animal, took up the pan and proceeded to ladle out ample helpings to the diners, who presumably were not too fastidious to refuse.

To follow a thresher was no sinecure. From the moment the great belt started to rotate between steam-engine and thresher, and the drum in the thresher itself began its loud monontonous hum, there was no respite. Sheaves were fed into the bowels of the machine with relentless regularity to

come out separated into corn, straw and chaff. Men ran up
granary steps carrying heavy sacks of grain. The lightest
but dirtiest job was collecting chaff or 'brot' which was used
for bedding. I sometimes fell for this task. At the end of the
day my clothing was impregnated with dirt and dust and
my eyes were red and sore. It was a relief to escape from the
continuous noise, to which I was unaccustomed.

In those days of late summer, if we finished in reasonable time Ronnie and I and a few other young chaps from
the neighbouring farms would go down to the River for a
swim before our supper. Our favourite spot was a natural
pool with the bank raised, at least on the opposite side.
Here I used to dive out over the rocks below, well out to
avoid skewering myself on the jagged edges just below the
surface. The contemplation of this exploit is enough to send
shudders through me now, but obviously at the time I
treated it as commonplace.

It was in the year of 1937 that I was able to make my own
contribution to the collection of anecdotes on Eccleston
Show. I was there, in the company of my Uncle Ben and at
his instigation I had my first glass of beer. Granted, I had
tasted it out of the barrel during hay-times at Land Hill,
but this was actually the first time that I ranged myself
alongside the men, and began the long delightful journey
towards ruin and eventual damnation. Or so it was considered by some men of God and various temperance
leagues.

According to the custom we saw little of the exhibits. My
Uncle Ben was too intent on making a 'bee-line' for the beer
tent. Mr. Walter Hull, a short stout gentleman with a very
florid face and protruding eyes very kindly offered to buy us
a drink. "What's Edwin having?", he enquired. My uncle
said that I should have a half of mild, out of the wood of
course. The beer tent was either too dull or it was over-
crowded, I forget which, so we moved to one of the pubs in
the village. There I was allowed another half and began to
feel a strange, agreeable sensation.

My Uncle Ben, now a little worse for drink, took himself

off to the gentlemen's lavatory. On his return, weaving rather unsteadily through the raucous crowd composed mainly of men, he had to pass a group of ladies who were receiving considerable attention. They deported themselves more freely than ever I had seen ladies behave, and were careless in the way in which they allowed their skirts to ride up over their knees as they sat on the high stools. Shy as I was at this totally unaccustomed lack of modesty, I could not prevent myself from casting surreptitious glances at the expanses of leg so displayed. Why was their dress so garish, and why did they wear so much powder and lipstick? In spite of the exaggerated crimson lips one or two were attractive, but the rest were older, more formidable, and resembled birds of prey. The seemed to smoke cigarettes incessantly. This habit, wholly acceptable for men, was wholly unacceptable for women in our village, as being common and immodest.

The young 'yokels' who were attracted to these ladies were almost as libidinous as the middle-aged lechers, especially the married ones who had gathered round, endeavouring to create the impression of male virility.

Though engaged in banter with the men and though enclosed by noise and bustle and smoke and figures constantly moving, these women were alert and vigilant. As my Uncle Ben returned from the lavatory, his 'mission' accomplished, one of them pointed to the front of his trousers and in a loud, shrill voice cried, "Your dorothy bag's open, love".

This remark was followed by a great burst of laughter from those round about.

I was mystified at the observation, which was explained by my uncle as he fastened his fly buttons. I was also embarrassed and not a little outraged. In the presence of these creatures I felt ill-at-ease, sensing that they might at any time turn their attention on to me and hold me up to ridicule. I was glad to escape.

Cycling home, taking care not to bump into each other,

for I was slightly unsteady and my Uncle Ben was worse, I questioned my uncle on the women in the pub.

For once my uncle was lost for words. He found it difficult to find adequate means of expression to explain the role of these women. As I have already said, sex in my family just did not exist. Obviously, being a countryman I knew about the birds and bees and about the basic functions of men and women in the act of procreation. There were also certain coarse and smutty remarks and stories which I had picked up. Innocent of such goings on, it would be two or three years before my own profession led me to places where these ladies made their livings.

My Uncle Ben did the best he could, but as his knowledge of such society was limited and academic it was unsatisfying. He muttered something about 'old bags' who had come from Blackpool or Preston seeking rich pickings. He admonished me not to consort with such as they, for fear of 'getting a dose'. This was highly unlikely, for had I known the haunts of these scarlet ladies, and had I had the poise and assurance to engineer an assignation with one of them, it would have come to nothing but unkind words, for I should have been unable to pay.

I went home with my uncle who had to change into his working clothes and return to Crane Hall to 'serve' or feed some calves and pigs in the late afternoon. I watched him as he lurched across the farmyard, a bucket of swill in each hand, and saw him disappear into the barn. I stayed in the yard, not wishing to get my clothes dirty.

The minutes ticked by and there was no sign of my uncle. Where on earth could he be? It was fortunate for me that the barn door was closed, for as I was opening it a savage beast of a dog flew at it, snarling most alarmingly. Through the crack in the door I could see my uncle spread-eagled on his back like the figure, recumbent and abandoned, in the cornfield in Brueghel's 'The Reaper'. Instead of a discarded wine-jug, his buckets lay beside him, one on each side where they had fallen. My uncle had succumbed to mid-day drinking to which he was unaccustomed. His snores reverb-

189

erated into the rafters. He remained oblivious to my shouts and to the growls and barks of his guardian 'hound of hell' which was trying its best to attack me.

After the corn had been gathered in, the mangolds were harvested. The full name for this root crop is 'mangold-wur-zel' with the alternative spelling 'mangel'. We called them mangels. Armed with machetes, Wind or Scroggins joined me as we went down the rows, bent double, pulling each mangel and trimming its base and 'snagging off' its leafy top in one movement. The ground-frost of early autumn was in the tops and our hands were raw and blue with cold. I probably suffered more because I was not as weathered as the others. (Snagging mangels on frosty mornings is a task I recommend be given to young felons with a weakness for attacking babies and old people). Long rows of purple-col-oured mangels lay behind us. Periodically we threw them into carts which moved slowly along, parallel to the rows. A great mound was formed near the farm buildings ready to be fed to the cattle in winter.

Sometimes I would stay at the farm overnight, some-times I would stay late in the evenings after work, when I would play the piano. Then I would launch myself into the darkness and cycle back to Hambleton.

There was a long drive, really more of a cart track, from Crane Hall Farm down to the main road which ran along by the river. On one side at least, woods overshadowed the track. It was quite a daunting prospect to set out in the dark down this track with its uneven surfaces and its grooves on either side, worn by generations of cart-wheels. The first part of the journey was made less appealing when I was told that it was haunted. Rawcliffe Hall was positiv-ely "wick wi' boggarts" — alive with them in fact, and there was this overspill on to Crane Hall property,

On this particular night it was very dark, darker than normal, with no moon at all. I only had a faint light run by a battery with very little power left in it. In the next year I would have a better lamp operated from a dynamo on the rear wheel. The carbide lamp had become obsolete.

I pointed my bicycle for home, standing on the pedals to achieve maximum speed, wishing to get to the open road as quickly as possible, when I could fly through the few other boggart-stretches on my way. Whatever route one chose there were always supernatural black-spots, especially though wooded stretches and at cross-roads and road-junctions, with never a street lamp to give temporary comfort to the lonely traveller. And the traveller was lonely. It was rare if I met anyone after about ten o'clock on that stretch of road.

About twenty yards down the track I had a shock which was enough to kill me. Suddenly with no warning at all I brushed against the whole length of a long hairy object. It first touched my hand which was grasping the handlebar and then met my leg. Every hair on my head stood bolt upright and a tremor ran through my body from the top of my head to the soles of my feet. It was soon over. As I made even more frantic efforts to gain speed and to keep my balance I heard the sound of hoofs galloping away from me on hard ground. It wasn't Satan come to claim me after all, but yet another donkey which was roaming loose. It was literally my last brush with donkeys and I never wanted another one.

The "sands were running out" for me at Crane Hall. I helped to dip sheep. Long days were spent with Ronnie cleaning out ditches and cutting hedges. The tasks of autumn were complete. All was safely gathered in. There was no more seasonal work to be done. It was with great reluctance that I had to move on.

The Passing Bell Tolls

I WENT back to Land Hill before Christmas to work as a full-time farm labourer. I had never lost touch, so it was really like going home.

In winter-time I travelled to and fro on my bicycle, but as the days lengthened, from February onwards, I ran over the fields to and from work. As dawn broke or before, I flung myself out of Ingol Cottage, up past Crooklands Cottage, my former home, and on through Mr. Will Hull's orchard and into the open pasture. I trespassed every time I went through the orchard, but as Mr. Will Hull did not live in the property attached and as he would not be anywhere near at the times when I made my journeys, there was no danger of discovery.

Mr. Hull is worthy of a book all to himself. When I was younger his presence was intimidating to me. He was fond of a glass or two of whisky to such an extent that his speech, hard enough to follow when he was sober because of his rapid staccato delivery, became incomprehensible to me when it was slurred.

Mr. Hull, who had attracted the curious nick-name 'Wavvers', was really kindly and harmless enough behind his somewhat blustery exterior. In my early teens I entered his workshop which was in the cottage beside the orchard. Only the brave, the foolhardy or the simple-minded entered this wretched place. It was an absolute certainty that when they left they would be in discomfort for some hours. The whole place, from top to bottom crawled with hen-lice. These fleas wer called 'fleff'. If a dog or other animal

scratched it was said to be 'fleffing itself'. One certainly
'fleffed oneself' on emerging from Mr. Hull's cottage.

Mr. Hull bought fowls which he executed, dressed and
took to market. His was a one-man cottage industry, although I daresay that at peak periods such as the week
before Christmas he would take on additional seasonal
labour. He would probably kill his birds by the simple
expedient of wringing their necks, which in the hands of an
expert is as humane as a killing can be. In this one room of
his little dwelling, once the comfortable living-room where
the respectable poor of previous generations had sat and
told their tales round the fireside, there was now extreme
neglect and squalor of unimaginable proportions. The air
was filled with dust, feathers and in their midst hordes of
panic-stricken fleffs in search of other hosts.

My Uncle Ben had acted as Mr. Hull's young part-time
assistant, so he knew all about this.

As Mr. Hull's arms flailed about plucking and now and
then ripping, the feathers descended to add yet another
layer to the deep carpet already there. Mr. Hull seemed to
be immune to ills which might have arisen from his distas-
teful but doubtless lucrative trade. As no Ministry of
Health officials worried him he was not concerned with
maintaining the highest standards of hygiene. If such authoritative folk already trod the earth none disturbed our
rustic tranquillity.

Mr. Hull disembowelled and dressed his own fowls.
Everything inedible such as heads, feet and entrails were
deposited on a midden in a corner of the orchard. Not only
did this noisome repository attract rats and vermin generally; domestic cats, exhibiting the curiosity of their kind
were wont to seek tit-bits from it. Our own cat, when we
were at Crooklands Cottage not far from Mr. Hull and the
midden, was not above paying a visit.

On quiet evenings sounds related to humans in distress
could be heard coming from the direction of the midden.
They were recognised by my grandmother as those of cats
being violently sick, with a possibility of our being among

their number. My grandmother poured recriminations on cats generally, and on Mr. Hull in his absence. More than once she met him face to face to give him the sharp edge of her tongue as he came tipsily past our garden gate on his way home from market and from the Shovels Inn.

In those days there were lots of flies, among them a large variety which we called a 'blow-fly'. I suspect that such depositories as those created by Mr. Hull afforded an ideal breeding-ground for these unwelcome visitors; that sudden onslaughts of diarrhoea and stomach upsets were directly attributable to them.

Having passed through the orchard I was soon on the top of the hill. In springtime I saw the sun rise directly ahead beind the foothills of the Pennines, twenty miles away in the distance. A mile away behind me lay my old friend the River, which latterly I had almost forsaken, shimmering in the light of the early morning. This hill-top, so my grandfather had said, from hearsay handed down, had been considered by John of Gaunt as a site for his castle, but he chose Lancaster instead.

Before me lay Land Hill with its trees and orchards enclosed by its stockade of hedges. In this enclosure and in the fields surrounding I was to labour strenuously until five or six o'clock at night with two short breaks for 'baggin' mid-morning and afternoon, and a longer one for the mid-day meal.

Sometimes I would pause briefly on top of the hill enjoying the solitude and the utter peace of the early morning countryside, when the world, reborn, rose fresh to meet another day. The crows pecked about in dew-laden pastures, always aware of my presence but not showing it. The hedges were filled with the singing of birds.

For me the simple still prevailed; the complex was just round the corner. I was still nature's child, would always be so. In spite of thin veneers of quasi-sophistication with which destiny would try to smear me I would only be truly content when I was wearing my peasant's hat.

Happiest when I was in such surroundings as I describe,

with great stretches of unspoilt land on either side of me as far as I could see, with only here and there a homestead. Happiest when I was using my physical strength which was developing rapidly into manhood. Why was it that I was not content to stay out my days, with one season rolling smoothly into another, one year extending to the next, with animals to tend and the knowledge that the cycle of sowing, growing and gathering would continue until I at last would die away and be gathered with my ancestors? The feeling that I was an integral part of the good earth and everything that grew and fed thereon was strong in me, an inheritance from the beginning of life itself. Yet the Demom was tugging at my sleeve, tugging more and more insistently, whispering more persistently in my ear that I must escape. Why had the Demon chosen to attack me and none of my rustic contemporaries? Yet attack me it did, with such ferocity that I fear that in this, my last year, I was sometimes a sullen and disagreeable workmate.

From the hill overlooking Land Hill I ran down into the valley, surmounting a stile or two on the way, before I began the slow climb up the footpath which stretched alongside the hedge to the crest of the long field. To the right of me was Stony End Pit where my grandfather had brought me, sacrificing a whole precious Saturday afternon, when I was six or seven years of age. Our intention was to catch perch.

Not many ponds round Hambleton were noted for perch, though there were roach in abundance. Tommy and I knew of at least one good place for perch fishing. When the broad beans were in flower or when the summer sky was heavy with thunder-clouds we would be off to Lewtas' Hill where there was a pond surrounded by a wide expanses of rushes. It required skill to drop our floats where we wanted them without our tackle becoming tangled. This pond was near to the one into which I had been pushed so ignominiously, close to the spot which Little Joe and I had selected for our successful experiment with the calcium carbide.

Big perch were said to live in Stony End Pit, though I was

never skilful enough to catch a really good one. On that day with my grandfather it was too hot and sunny. Our sole catch was a perch about five inches long, but it was, nevertheless, an exciting adventure for me.

My tired old grandfather with the end of his journey already in sight bore the improvised rod and tackle whilst I, lively, my life still to begin, my only thought for present pleasures, pranced beside him, bearing homeward the fish on a rush which my grandfather had threaded through the gills. My grandmother, complying to my plea as usual, cooked the fish in butter in a little dish in the oven and I ate it for my supper.

Just as memories must have invaded my grandfather's mind as he sat beside me by the Pit, familiar ground for him, so now there were memories for me.

Work done at the farm, I would retrace my steps. It was no effort to me, that mile or two at the end of a day's toil. As the sun had travelled round, the day had grown tired, but not I. Just as I had watched the sun rise twelve hours before, so I watched it setting in early spring. Except on very rare occasions when there had been two or three late nights in a row, I was not weary. There were tales a-plenty of aching limbs, sore feet, mysterious maladies, general debility from the older folk who surrounded me but for me, at this the beginning of my golden age, I never understood any of them or knew what it was to be really tired.

It is obvious that to give me such sustained energy, to keep me in trim, I needed constant nourishment. If I have drooled about the meals at the Critchley's, it must be stated emphatically that my drooling in no way detracts from Margaret's cuisine at Land Hill. I suppose that as Land Hill had been my second home for years, Mrs. Critchley's table, seating more and holding more was a novelty in a bigger setting.

Among the vast quantity of victuals which Arthur and I, still growing, 'shovelled' away, two dishes excel. One, prepared and served in season by Margaret by special request was nothing less than a triumph; the other, provided by

Tom, who only took over as cook out of dire necessity was anything but.

Margaret's speciality was a pudding, a big , rich, juicy pudding in which carbohydrates predominated. The only restriction on its size was the size of the oven. Arthur and I sat spell-bound, saliva filling our mouths, as Margaret inverted the pudding basin on to a large plate, revealing the great outer layer of suet, all shiny and greasy, with blackberry juice beginning to seep through in places. The pudding, as you will have gathered, was packed with succulent blackberries, fresh picked. If Arthur and I did collect a few extra carbohydrates they did not stay with us for long. After three helpings each, about all we young trenchermen could manage, we sat back and puffed a bit after the manner of adults of more generous build, then flung ourselves out to work it all off.

Every once in a while Margaret would crave to escape from house-wifely duties, to take a peep at the world beyond. The Ribble bus bore her away to far distant places with quaint names — Bacup and Todmorden — to relatives who lived there. I took little interest. I had only been as far as Preston, once on a day-trip with the school to see a liner at Liverpool, once for a few days to Southport with Margaret and Arthur. What mattered was that we three males were left to fend for ourselves which meant that Tom appointed himself, automatically with no preliminary discussions whatsoever, as house-keeper-cum-cook.

His cookery book, had it been published, would not have met with universal approbation. It contained one recipe, even less-demanding and challenging than the much-quoted boiling of an egg which comes traditionally at the bottom of cooking skills. Only two ingredients, three if you count a spoonful of sugar, were needed. They were bread and milk. Milk we had a-plenty, gallons of it on tap, only a few yards from the back door. Never a great advocate of this natural beverage, I suppose it was now that I formed a positive loathing for it. The "staff of life" was stacked on a slab in the pantry, enough to withstand a siege. But if you can imagine a big, steaming basin of bread and milk, standing to attention waiting to be consumed at every meal, morning, noon and night, you will understand why I developed ever-increasing tremors of revulsion.

Fortunately, Margaret's absences were never for long, but they were long enough.

I suppose cows were my speciality. As soon as I arrived at the farm I started work. There were no preliminaries, no standing around braziers and drinking tea like council workers were apt to do after my grandfather's time. It was straight into the range to fodder the cows with hay and to prepare the feed to put into their wooden troughs. Each cow had its own which was given to it whilst it was being milked.

I must confess that I might have snatched a drink at the watering-trough as soon as I had arrived. This watering-trough stood over at the other side of the yard from the entrance. It was made of wood and was raised on legs. It served to water all the stock on the farm when they were laid up in winter. They had to be let out in relays and supervised. Watering was a longish process and meant extra work at this time of year.

Fungi lined the sides of the trough and a few fish swam about in its depths. Midges and other insects settled on the surface and there was always a thin film on it which could be seen when the sun shone on it. Parasites, hair and particles of food would drop off the cattle as they drank. When I blew into the water to make a clear space before I drank, I never gave a thought for all these impurities, nor for the deposits of fish excrement which the water must have contained. I never suffered any ill-effects whatsoever, even though I drank copiously from that trough several times in a working day.

I think it amused Pa and Arthur to see me drinking alongside the bull. The bull lived alone in a small pen which was warm and well protected from bad weather. As he was an expensive animal with a responsible job to do, he was given the best of attention. It is a pity that I cannot remember his name, for I grew close to him.

When it was seen that a rapport had been established between myself and the bull I was given sole charge of his welfare. I fed, groomed and watered him and led him out on his bull-staff when a cow or heifer was waiting to be served. It was not long before he greeted me with his bellow the moment he heard me enter the yard, so I took to feeding him before I joined Arthur to attend to the cows. If I had a moment to spare I brushed him until he shone. He rewarded me with his affection. I knew that bulls could turn on one and that I must always be aware of him. That is why I took the precaution of using the stout bull-staff which clipped on to the ring in his nostrils, allowing me, if I needed, to keep im at arm's length.

For me he was always a gentle bull who never gave me cause for alarm. There was one occasion, however, when he did put me through my paces. I took him out to serve a cow which was calling for him impatiently from a nearby field where the herd was out at grass. It was a mistake. We should have brought her into the yard as we always did, but this time for some reason now forgotton 'Pa' had made the decision that we should go to the cow.

The bull, in his haste to placate one of his partners, ran away. Who could blame him. On such an errand I would have done the same. Even with this end in view I could not have achieved nearly the same speed. I clung tightly to the staff and was hurled along with my body at times parallel to the ground and a couple of feet above it. Here and there one foot or the other touched the earth momentarily. I was aware of the cries of Arthur and his father coming even more faintly from the distance, urging me to hang on. I was surprised to find that I was still with my friend the bull when he performed his function, for it had all happened so quickly. When all passion was spent, which did not take long, we walked back at a sedate pace. We both visited the trough, blew the surface clean simultaneously and took cooling drinks together.

Later, when I had been away from the farm for over a year and returned on a short visit, the bull raised his head and gave me his old greeting when he heard me arrive. Here was one who had not forgotten me.

After milking, a process which had to be done twice a day, first thing in the morning and in the late afternoon, which I have described in a previous chapter, we would go in to breakfast in the warm, friendly kitchen with its old-fashioned range and open fire. It was much smaller than the one at Crane Hall and was used as a living-room. Arthur and I, still growing lads, were forever hungry and Margaret must have had a hard job to keep up with us.

Arthur with his dogs, at Land Hill in late 1930's.

Monotonous, repetitive tasks, which taxed the strength beyond the normal level or which caused discomfort, or momentary contentment, are all I suppose, worthy of re-call.

Mucking out was a monotonous task, carried out at least once daily. The large wooden barrow was filled, wheeled to the midden (not without difficulty over the cobbled yard), and tipped on it. In fine weather it was tolerable but in the rain or even worse, ice and snow, it was far from comfort-able. When the midden had grown sufficiently an addi-tional challenge was added to the obstacle course. The barrow had to be run up a plank before it was emptied.

The manure had to be carted to the fields. The cart, positioned close to the midden with the horse waiting pa-tiently in the shafts, was filled by swinging fork-ful after fork-ful until there was enough to make a load. Then it was off to the field with it. On arrival the tailboard was removed and the manure was raked out with a muck-rake into heaps spaced at intervals and in line. If the ground was sodden, care had to be taken not to get stuck. Once, with old Tinker, I had a mishap. He sank to his knees in a soggy patch when the cart was fully-laden. I had to rake off enough of the load to enable me to lift the shafts and get the weight off his back. It needed some effort and I had to work fast.

I do see myself, however, on a beautiful sunny afternoon, standing on a load of hay and reaching it on to the 'moo' which was rising in the Dutch barn. Bare from the waist-up, bronzed by exposure, for I had my shirt off whenever I could, I swung my pitchfork and rejoiced in the day, the setting, the sweet smell of young hay and especially in my health and strength, in this my last hay-time at Land Hill Farm.

I watch myself, alone, remote from the farm, tackling a high hawthorn hedge which has grown wild and is badly in need of cutting back. I lop it down to about four feet, cut out all the old wood and lay the sturdy growth remaining, staking as I go along. I have a fire going and as I move along I burn the debris. 'Pa' who had already demonstrated on hedges with considerable patience has "given me my head". He has never come to watch me work. I am summoned to my meals or to milking by his characteristic piercing whistle or by Arthur's Tarzan cry. The farm lies a half-a-mile away. When I have almost finished the hedge 'Pa' turns up to inspect, spits out a stream of tobacco juice (for he is well away from Margaret's observation) and says "Tha's done a good job, Ned". It is praise indeed and I swell with pride inwardly.

I owe a lot to Tom of Land Hill. In many skills he was expert and insisted on a good job being done. I think of him and smile wryly when I pass badly-cut hedges or see people, unskilled or apathetic, taking great bites with their shears. It is as if rats had 'chattered' away and left great uneven gaps.

Once I was loaned out like any other farm implement. I might have been a mowing-machine or a chain-harrow, but I wasn't. I just happened to be an efficient mucker-out-of-shippons. The previous evening Jackie Bailey of Clay Gap Farm, husband of Bell who was the eldest daughter of Jonathan, and therefore my mother's cousin, had visited Land Hill to bargain with Tom for my services for a few days. Whether Jackie's farm-hand had found the pressure too much and had fled, or whether he was ill through over-work is lost to posterity. All I knew was that next morning, after milking and breakfasting at Land Hill, I shot off on my bike to Clay Gap, three or four minutes away.

Jackie Bailey, of Clay Gap — Mr. Bailey to the likes of serfs such as me — was a quaint little man, not unlike my Great-uncle Tom in facial appearance. He would have passed well as a garden gnome had he been a little shorter in stature. Mr. Bailey would not have liked this description, for like most small men he possessed an abundance of bluster, swagger, pomposity and apparent confidence. He walked very quickly as if every second had to be accounted for. His conversation, monosyllabic in the main, was delivered in short, harsh outbursts. He was not the most articulate of men.

He could not have created a restful presence in the big farm-house which he shared, for want of a better word, with Bell, in drab surroundings bordering on discomfort. Mr. Bailey, who had succeeded his father Dickie at Clay Gap, was notorious for keeping an extremely firm grip on his purse-strings.

It was here that the servant-man had tossed in fever, lying on the bare boards of the landing under his covering of sacks, gulping down a 'lading-can' of water during the lonely hours of the night. It was here that Peggy Bowman had lived her short, tragic life. The hasty, selfish actions of a heartless father had caused her departure from this life at a pitifully early age. As I worked away in the shippon, scooping up from the 'group' with my big shovel the manure which was on the runny side, for Jackie was as sparing with his straw as he was with everything else, I thought about poor Peggy. I could almost sense her troubled spirit gazing sadly down from the rafters on me, her direct descendant, separated by five generations and one hundred and thirty years in time, assessing how I measured up to the old Bowman line.

How did the story go. I had heard it told often enough over fire-sides both at home and at Land Hill. Her misfortune had survived the passing of time, had been transmitted well nigh intact.

Peggy had been born in 1802. She also had been comely enough to attact a suitor, a legendary character called 'Sil' Cooper. Could Sil be short for Silas? I rather hoped so, for from the very little that was known of him he presented a lonely, individualistic, wandering spirit which identified with that of 'Silas Marner'.

Sil had travelled on foot from a place unknown beyond the River Wyre. He had forded the river at low tide for there was no bridge then, and had made his slow progress through that part of the Fylde, passing Shard and Hambleton and presumably Bickerstaff on his way. His journey must perforce have been slow, for he led a cow by its 'halter', an offering to be made to Peggy's father when Sil asked for

Peggy's hand in marriage. He gave every impression of being an honourable man, this Sil Cooper.

John Bowman, Peggy's father, was 'in his cups' when Sil arrived. Drink intervened, shattering the promise of future happiness, wrecking utterly at least one life, marring the early life of one yet unborn. Sil's overture to Peggy's father was greeted with derision ending in an action which could only be interpreted as contempt. John Bowman threw his hat at Sil at the same time uttering loud, offensive imprecations. Without further ado, seemingly without any effort made to placate the irascible John, Sil turned about and returned the way he came, still trailing his docile beast behind him.

With the ardent pleas of his sweetheart still ringing in his ears, Sil made his solitary way back to the river and across it, disappearing into the mysterious countryside from whence he came and simultaneously into history.

Whether he salved his disappointment through a new love, or whether he sat lonely at his fireside until old age at last overtook him is not recorded. Nor is it known whether he was aware that his disconsolate lover was carrying his child. Yet it was so.

In 1823 Richard Bowman, Peggy's son, was born. Four years later, at the age of twenty-five, Peggy died, it was said of a broken heart. This John Bowman did not show the same compassion that his namesake was to show to another bastard child some hundred years later, that child being me.

Though the details are so obscure as to be almost non-existent, one deduces a cold, grey atmosphere prevailing at Clay Gap, broken by outbursts of resentment and bad temper. It was as if 'Wuthering Heights' had been lifted bodily across the Pennines to the sometimes equally forbidding flat-lands of the Fylde.

Richard, born in shame and rejected by John his grandfather, may have been fortunate when he was, to use my Uncle Ben's apt Victorian expression, "thrown on to the world". A Mr. Shakeshaft, whose origins are totally unresearched, befriended the boy and brought him up as his own. Of course, Richard survived, he being the great-grandfather who came to hold a respected position in village society as the farmer of Moss Side Farm and the sire of or eleven children born in wedlock.

Moss Side Farm where my Great Grandfather lived.

What manner of man was Sil Cooper? His genes, now less concentrated, lurked about in my body, part of me, passed down in an unbroken chain. I could easily turn and walk away had I met with a similar rebuff, but whether I could have forsaken a sweetheart with whom I had united in passion is hard to say.

Bell, Jackie's wife, came into the shippon and my reverie was dispelled. Peggy was gone, and young Richard with her; Sil Cooper was gone and with him his cow; old vindictive John was gone. They had receded into the shadows where they were to stay until I, writing some fifty years later was to resuscitate them. It was a familiar enough drama, insignificant save for those who had enacted it.

As Bell stood before me I thought what a hopeless woebegone figure she presented. She had been good-looking once, so it was said, but not a vestige remained. All her femininity was gone. Her face was lined and drawn, she wore a wrap-round pinafore and thick woollen stockings which were wrinkled. The most unattractive part of her dress was her clogs which were large and crude. They caused her to walk badly and to move slowly. Long years of relentless toil, dragging great buckets of pig-swill across the rough, uneven cobbles of the farm yard had caused her to stoop and to age prematurely. There was another reason for her posture. Under her wrap-round pinafore was a sinister secret, unknown to anyone, probably her husband included. Bell dragged about with her a monstrous double-hernia worsening all the time and, of course, untreated. I never did find out whether her condition was revealed shortly before her death or whether it was laid bare only when she herself was being prepared for burial.

Bell had brought me my 'drinking', my mid-morning refreshment. In this instance there was a pint mug of tea and a large piece of egg custard.

"Ee Edwin", she said, shaking her head, her voice full of tremulous concern, "what is a lad with your education doing in a job like this?"

Did she foresee for me nothing but mucking out shippons, drudgery poorly-paid (I was getting about twelve shillings a week with my meat at the time), with nothing at the end of it? What reply could I give? I leant against the shippon wall, ate my custard and drank my tea. My hands were none too clean. Such refinements as 'scrubbing up' at every opportunity were left to 'townies' who did not appreciate the pleasures which close proximity to an assortment of animal excrement could bring. My clogs were caked in manure and if the truth were told, a drop or two would have infiltrated and impregnated my stockings.

I felt no remorse, no self-pity, no humility. I had next to no money, no possessions apart from my clothes and my bicycle, but I did not feel deprived.

Once more I filled my big, clumsy wooden barrow with its wooden wheel and metal rim and pushed it across the cobbles to the midden and up the plank. Afterwards I fed and foddered the animals, cut some hay with a hay-spade and, to Bell's relief, fed the pigs. My stint of loaned-out serfdom over, I was happy enough to depart from Clay Gap Farm, back to my muck-spreading. There was too much tragedy built into its walls for a young chap like me, too much brooding melancholy present for me to tackle with any degree of equanimity.

It was better when I was by myself in the lower meadow, away from everyone, where I could be alone with my thoughts, where the Demon did not tug so hard. It was whilst I was so occupied, with the not unpleasant smell of manure rising from the good earth and incidentally giving me an appetite, with Land Hill dozing on the hillside, not yet folded in its green summer cloak, that I heard the passing bell toll. It was a familiar enough sound, sonorous and solemn, reminding us all of our mortality or immortality, according to our way of thinking. It reached out over several square miles from the tower of Hambleton Church, just across the fields from where I was.

Always we knew for whom the bell tolled, unless there had been an unexpected fatality. This time it was for Mr. Salisbury, a farmer of formidable bearing and great conviction, who had visited my grandfather frequently during his last illness.

As was the custom of all peasants who toiled out their long days in the fields, surrounded by nature and exposed to all her rigours, I paused, leant on my fork and gave a thought for his passing. It was not until long afterwards that I realised that for me, this fleeting moment when the passing bell tolled had a much greater significance. It had tolled symbolically, in a much wider sense had been an ominous signal for the end of my youth and the death of my village as I had known it.

A Visionary Tour

COULD I have been given supernatural power in spring 1938 to have projected myself fifty years onwards, I should have been brought up with a jolt at the appearance of Land Hill. Tall, unsightly angular buildings would stand out against Land Hill's perimeter, with no effort made to match the natural colours of the countryside. Seen from Hambleton churchyard they would obtrude even more prominently, symbols of modern industrialised farming, governed by carefully balanced calculations and pulled hither and thither at the whims of the pundits of the E.E.C. Hen cabins would be gone, or remain only as rotting woebegone monuments, with no hens roaming far and wide in the pastures picking about for nutritious tit-bits, feathers ruffled side-ways in the wind. Stony End Pit would be gone, where my grandfather and I had sat on that sunny afternoon, where Arthur and I had sailed our home-made boats and where I had braved the depths and swum across from one shingly side to the other. Now it was filled in, a collecting place for rubbish. No sun-lit waters permitted glimpses of perch, once considered permanent residents of their ancestral home.

In this late twentieth century, already looking into the twenty-first, not so much with pleasurable anticipation as with foreboding, how would my great-grandfather have fared, who knowing no other, had been well content with his small-holding at Moss Side, very near to 'Aunt Mary's' cottage, virtually self-supporting but ever on the brink of penury. My mother, when she was a little girl at the turn of the century, had memories of him at his breakfast, sitting close to a fire already gleed, enjoying his mug of tea and hot toast well buttered. The bread baked on his own hearth would be from his own flour, the butter from his own cow. It sounds idyllic but to him it was reality, more often than not grim reality. Yet there is no evidence to refute the belief that he was satisfied with what he had and sought for nothing more. Now, almost one hundred years on a very different philosophy prevailed. Few were now content with either their station or their chattels and craved for more.

From what I can gather from my Uncle Ben, my great-grandfather must have grown corn as well as potatoes, for there is mention of 'windles of wheat' being taken to Hambleton Peg Mill to be ground into flour. Each windle weighed two hundred-weights, which would need some 'humping' about. The mill, so named because its structure could be rotated to set the sails to the prevailing wind, stood on Mill Lane almost opposite the track which led to Moors Farm. It ceased to function in 1902 after being damaged in a storm, and gradually fell into decay. My great-grand-father, who rented and worked half-a-dozen turf-dales on Rawcliffe Moss, not only used turfs of peat for his own fuel, but also traded in this commodity. One of his customers was the miller who needed peat to dry the grains of oats, wheat and barley. There can be little doubt that a barter system existed between the two of them.

The rectangular wedges of peat, cut out and laid to dry in summer months, were brought home to be built into turf-stacks, ready for the winter. Turf-stacks were familiar enough features when I was a boy. We always had one or two loads delivered in the autumn when we were at Crooklands Cottage and Ingol Cottage. Awaiting the arrival of the peat and assisting in raising the cylindrical stacks was always an exciting incident in my young life.

To return to my stationary position in the field, taking advantage of my futuristic vision, I should note with some amazement that the churchyard had extended to twice its original size in these fifty years, indicating an unusual increase in population. It was beyond all proportion to that which must have remained fairly static for at least a century or two previously, if not for longer. Names alien to the old familiar ones hitherto tabulated were inscribed on the gravestones, indicating indisputably an 'invasion' of some considerable size.

Hambleton Council School, now known as Hambleton County Primary School, no less, remained externally unchanged save for an unsightly bicycle-shed which had been placed across its frontage, successfully spoiling an agreeable Victorian edifice. Furthermore, rectangular 'pustules' had appeared at the side and in what had been the playground at the back, seemingly dropped haphazardly from the sky, embarrassing further the dignity of the old building.

The demand for these extensions must only have meant a greater number of pupils on roll. But where were the children? I saw no youngsters at play as I glided up the Village and over the hill to Market Street. There were ghosts, yes. My grandmother in the pleated white bonnet which was a characteristic part of her uniform, stood at the corner by Ingol Cottage, looking down the Village, anxious for my safety when I had gone to the wars. My great-uncle, easily recognisable by the carelessness of his dress and his outrageous hat, laboriously made his way home. A group of children, Harry Catterall, Little Joe and myself included, rushed about in the gathering dusk, shrill voices crying out in excitement, striving to capture every moment of playing-time before darkness fell. Now there was a strange unnatural silence, with all the young folk indoors, bleeping away at computer-games or staring entranced at television programmes of dubious value. The ad-men had gained a captive audience. No longer were former melodies recognized as creations of great masters, but as tunes which accompanied advertisements for cereals or dog food or toilet paper.

The Village itself had become transformed since my day. Where little more than hand-to-mouth survival had ruled for the majority there had arisen an atmosphere of opulence. The dwellings, previously for the most part reasonably maintained in a utilitarian manner had now become festooned with stylised extras. There was, however, little fear of the old type of inquisitorial easing back of curtains, for people did not know each other as in the old days. Individuality had been replaced by impersonality and interest was now only centred upon one's self. To be fair there was still a nucleus of 'natives' as opposed to 'locals', loyal to tradition, but their number was diminishing.

An old barn once housing old and rusty farm implements on which hens roosted and left their droppings, had become a reconstruction of rustic domesticity with all modern conveniences. Ingol Cottage, once angular and commonplace with no external romantic appeal in spite of its name, which implied thatched eaves, white-washed walls and a garden of wild flowers, now took the breath away with its splendour. It had been extended and its facade so skilfully treated that it was comparable to matrons of mature age who now remained perennially young through cosmetic surgery and the application of artifices for which they could well afford to pay. Bending over 'dolly-tubs', whirling 'dolly-legs' round and round or beating 'possers' up and down was out; women no longer looked wizened and wrinkled, spent and worn come the menopause.

At the passing of my youth, most families in the main streets which led from one end of the Village to the other were poor. Some, and mine was one — even if my mother would deny it — had, as the saying goes, "scarcely two ha'pennies to rub together". There were those who were well off or reasonably so, others who were dragging themselves upwards by dint of thrift and hard work, but the tilt was towards poverty rather than riches. Now it was as if a treasure trove had cascaded on the Village. Heralding its coming, electricity had arrived in 1934, so I witnessed its coming, although I could not have prophesied the potential it promised. Street-lighting had been installed as late as 1960, so like all my contemporaries and all before me, I had been accustomed to move about in darkness. No-one was assaulted and women and girls were free to come and go. It was considered a shameful thing anyway, at least in rural areas where such principles were still upheld, to even consider taking advantage of a woman's relative weakness. Children could travel to and from school, even as darkness fell in winter, with very little fear of violation or harassment.

With the advent of electricity, most or even all the pre-occupation with the supernatural had been swept away. Ghosts, as everyone knew, receded at cock-crow which announced the dawn. They were not normally disposed to work in the full light of day. They shared this habit with vampires, though I never heard of a Hambleton vampire. So startled were these wraiths at the instant, bright light which resulted from the operation of a switch, that they who had caused terror for centuries were now themselves so terror-stricken that they had fled, never to return. The boggarts, like those they had haunted and with whom they had formed such a close relationship had all gone. How would my Great-uncle Dick have survived in a world devoid of phantoms? And what would there be to talk about on the long winter evenings?

On the edges of the Village had sprung 'rabbit-warrens' of streets with little houses and bungalows each in its own small enclosure. Suburbia had come. Catterall's field, once meadow-land or pasture overlooking Ryecroft Corner, had long been a housing estate. West Lodge across the road, once the impressive residence of my Great-uncle Jonathan, with whom my Great-uncle Ben had lived and grown his tomatoes and large onions and had fought a losing battle with his reluctant limbs, was now a complex of shops, with what had been the large lawn and flower-beds now an asphalt covered parking-space. Further up the road past Shovels Inn the earthen paths which had led to Bunker's were now metalled roads with the expensive well-kept dwellings of Hambleton's new population everywhere to be seen. The Cop and the Cut were no longer private places. A fence had been built round my old diving platform at the head of the Cut to discourage latter-day divers from plunging in. Apart from the fact that it was overlooked by residences which positively shrieked affluence, the River was said to be polluted, a common enough condition in these times, and that it was hazardous to bathe in its waters.

On the other side of the Village the same expansion had occurred. The former Reading Room expanded and transformed from mediocrity, had all the appearance of a country club where prosperous celebrities with ample time on their hands assembled to exchange G & T's and discuss jet-setting holidays in Tenerife, Cyprus or Yugoslavia or wherever was in fashion at the moment.

Up Church Lane, going towards the school and church, yet another of Catterall's fields had been sacrificed for more houses and bungalows, more mazes of streets. It was hard to recapture in this new setting a memorable scene which I had witnessed one Sunday morning on this same stretch of pasture which had gone. I would be about fourteen and was on my way to the morning service, when Catterall's boar, no respecter of either morals or the Lord's Day had chosen to serve a sow in full view of church-goers. Unlike the cliques of ageing ladies of pious dispositions who averted their eyes or went through the motions, I watched the act in all its basic splendour, enjoying the grunts of animal passion and the slow movements of the boar. The two participants were engrossed in the act of procreation, whilst we were on our way to reflect sombrely on the life hereafter.

It was with nothing short of awe that an hour or so later, on my way home, I found that the two pigs were still copulating, more slowly but still with evident enjoyment. This display of sexual control left such a lasting impression that from then onwards it was my dearest wish that should I be destined to return to life in another form it should be as a boar.

The ever-increasing burden of traffic flowing from Blackpool, the Las Vegas of the North, and from the industrial town of Preston, had meant a constant improvement in road systems. Business men and traders, retired or still working, jaded and suffering from stress — a late twentieth century malady — had sought refuge in this haven which had formerly been overlooked or scorned.

Possibly the change was reflected most in the pubs. Now each had lost its former identity and was like most others. The old solid wooden structures round the bars, the glass partitions, had been ripped out long ago and fashionable, garish furnishings had replaced them. Who was to blame the landlords? As in all other parts of the country it was the young who supported such establishments. Commercially the most gullible of society, the needs of the young were of primary concern. One would be very fortunate to meet one resident who had been there in the time of one's own youth. Even the invaders themselves had been over-run by hordes of inquisitive visitors intent on savouring the atmosphere of quaint country hoselries which, of course, were anything but.

My visionary tour would be incomplete were I to omit one last reference to the profusion of mechanically-propelled vehicles which covered the earth like great writhing swarms of multi-coloured insects which had reached plague-like proportions. To and fro they flitted in restless profusion, these indispensible life-support systems on wheels, paradoxically creating as much stress in one way as they did in alleviating it in another.

The Demon Wins

A DECISIVE action which was to shape my destiny was made in May, 1938. I joined the Territorial Army and became a gunner in a Field Artillery Unit which had its headquarters in a drill hall not far from South Shore Station, Blackpool. As I was considered to be more educated than some, I was assigned to the survey section at the Command Post of the Battery. I was the rawest recruit and remained so during my stay with the 'Terriers'.

In another trade or profession I would have been a tea-boy. Once more it was I who was draped in containers; it was I who carried the 'Director', which was a kind of theodolite.

Once or twice a week I attended for 'drill' or training, which meant little more for me than a perfunctory consultation of certain numerical tables published by the Ministry of Defence, or watching the established members play snooker, a game in which I took very little interest. A couple of times I went out on a training exercise to the grounds of a stately home at Lytham St. Annes where I assembled the equipment and stood by whilst others took readings. We ate our haversack rations. A little gentle gun- drill was demonstrated just to show willing. Then towards evening we limbered up, climbed into the lorries and trundled off home.

There were some murmurs of protest back at the farm when I had to take time off on a Sunday. These protests became full-voiced when it was known that I must be absent for a full fortnight in August to go to practice camp. I must confess that it was a blow to them, for I believe that in that year hay-time was late and there was still some hay to gather when I went to camp. However, duty called. The

'King's summons' could not be ignored. I helped to load guns and equipment on to a special train at Talbot Road Station, and we chugged off to Northumberland and the artillery range at Redesdale, near Otterburn.

There is a photo still in existence, taken outside Ingol Cottage, when I was about to set out on what to me was a great adventure. It shows a tall, thin youth in uniform, which includes riding breeches, puttees and spurs, by then mainly obsolete in the new mechanised Army. It is a picture of which I am not proud. Apart from the ill-fitting tunic, at the sight of which regimental tailors in the 'Regulars' would have protested in the strongest terms, and apart from my un-soldier-like stance which could not be otherwise, for I had done no 'square-bashing' whatsoever, the position of the peaked cap makes me writhe for it is set at a rakish angle. It was, of course, placed in this way deliberately in imitation of heroes of the Silver Screen, who always wore their head-gear in this way and incidentally, still do. I was ignorant of the knowledge that any squad-sergeant at the Depot R.A., Woolwich, would have screamed in fury at such desecration and would have jumped up and down and dashed his stick violently to the ground, before 'falling in' two men to have me escorted to the guardroom in double quick time.

My ignorance was not confined to the regulations governing service dress. Already eighteen, I had rarely been further than a line drawn on the map joining Blackpool, Preston, Lancaster and Fleetwood, a twenty mile radius from Hambleton.

The chaps I was with at Redesdale were a good bunch. Some of them had been Regulars, not necessarily in the R.A. There was one I remember well who had been in the Royal Signals. These old soldiers were easily recognisable by their bearing and turn-out and by their professionalism in handling routine matters. They knew all the tricks when it came to making themselves comfortable. It was they who took me under their wings and showed me how to organise my kit and how to lay it out for inspection; how to regulate my bed-space in the bell-tent we were in, and most import-ant, how to make my bed, using groundsheet and a couple of blankets.

They also took me to the canteen. This fortnight at camp was the annual holiday for these chaps and they made the most of it. The N.A.A.F.I. was well patronised. Now I was raised to that macho-male level in society where half-pints were pushed aside in favour of pint measures.

During the past few months I had taken to visiting Blackpool once a week with Ronnie Critchley, on the pillion seat of his motor-cycle. We would drop into a pub for a half-pint, possibly two, but never more. Now I was in the midst of the hardcore, with pint glasses of mild or bitter set up in advance, covering the N.A.A.F.I. table, still waiting to be drunk. I did not get drunk, nor did anyone force drink on me. Yet it must be confessed that I went back to my quarters in the bell-tent in a very happy state several times in that fortnight.

The women who served at the counter were known as "N.A.A.F.I. tarts", an unkindly all-embracing description which was probably slanderous, for some of them would be respectable employees in the centre of what was then an establishment populated solely by men. My eyes were op-ened so wide that they almost left their sockets at the matter-of-fact way these female attendants accepted the most ribald songs without seemingly batting an eyelid. I suppose it was yet another example of familiarity breeding contempt. Again, I was bound to make comparisons, as I had done in my observance of the 'professionals' in the pub at Great Eccleston. What would have been my mother's reaction, for instance, or that of the ladies who supervised stalls at our Sunday School's bring and buy sales, or most contrasting of all, that of the matrons and modest young women who decorated our church for the harvest festival?

One after the other the old soldiers rose to their feet and sang to the assembly. Everyone joined in the choruses. Nostalgia was very evident. I began to learn something about the intense loneliness and longing of men who had been sent far away from home to soldier in a hot climate for a number of years.

There were the old favourites like 'Ramona' and 'Souvenirs'. There was 'My Brother Sylvest' who had a load of forty medals on his chest.

Words not used in polite conversation were substituted for those in the 'straight' version without the least sign of self-consciousness.

> *"'Ave you 'eard of the old trooper's that's leaving*
>   *Bombay,*
> *Bound for old Blighty shores,*
> *Heavily laden with time expired men,*
> *Bound for the land they adore.*
> *There's many a bloke should have been on that boat,*
> *There's many a c— signing on.*
> *Soldiering on for a tora buckshee,*
> *That's what I call f——g hard lines".*

It was with awe and tremendous enjoyment that I listened to these ditties and formed a lasting companionship with the men who sang them.

There was one composition which went right through the alphabet, disclosing the skills and technical terms, some now becoming obsolete, which were appropriate only to Gunners.

> *"A is for Artillery to which we belong,*
> *B is for Battery so brave and so strong,*
> *C is for Corrector we put on the Fuse*
> *And D is for Drag-ropes which all Gunners use.*
> *Sing high, sing low, wherever you go,*
> *The boys of the R.A. they never say No".*

With lads of my own age or thereabouts, and there were several of them, splendid fellows, I went over the moors and swam in the pond-like stretches which I think were part of a river. We dived and sky-larked about as young men will. The water, even at this time of year was very cold, but it did not deter us from enjoying ourselves.

All in all, my first excursion beyond the confines of my own territory was highly instructive. It was inevitable that having had an attraction for the Army in the first place, and having now enjoyed my brief experience of it, I would want to become a professional soldier.

When I returned home I was still more unsettled and was not proud of my bad temper which I barely disguised to those at Land Hill. It was uncharacteristic of me, a temporary phase which I had to live through and which I was soon to shed.

At Christmas, lying in front of the fire on the settee at Ingol Cottage, watching the flames leap and dance, I knew that I must leave all the comforts which I had. I also knew that I was a fool, and a selfish one at that. My grandmother would be heart- broken and so would my mother. There was no going back. The Demon, who never left me alone, had decided.

On 8th February, 1939, I travelled by bus to Lancaster and went straight to the Barracks. It was no a social call. Before long I was on the return journey, formalities completed. The medical officer had passed me A1, the documents had been filled in and signed. The King's Shilling had been proffered and accepted. I was now in the Regular Army as a recruit gunner in the Royal Regiment of Artillery, Field Branch. My engagement was for six years with the Colours and six with the Army Reserve — in short 'six and six'. My army paybook states that I was 5ft. 11ins. tall and weighed 140lbs.

Given only a few days' grace, I served out my week at the farm. Almost before I knew it I was on my way to the Depot R.A., Woolwich, S.E.18. The indispensible and faithful Ronnie took me to Lancaster on that dour February morning. As in a dream I watched the countryside speed past as I sat in the train, south-bound for London. Like a latter day 'Dick Whittington' I was in search of fame and fortune.

I was familiar with the songs which had come out of the First World War, even 'Goodbye, Dolly Grey' which was from the Boer War. My mother, going about her housework, would suddenly burst into song and become even more industrious. It was then that she would be recalling the young men who had been snatched so dramatically from her young life, depriving her of love and companionship both then and in the long years ahead.

"There's a silver lining, through the dark cloud shining,
Turn the dark cloud inside out, till the boys come home".

Her boy was gone. The little cottage was empty at his passing. The fields and hedgerows, the copses and country lanes, the river, would seldom see him again. He had chosen a new bed and there, henceforth, he must lie. May-time would enfold the fair land with greenery. Hay-time would come, then harvest. Leaves would fall and winter set in, but he would not be there to see.

He had torn himself from his family, betrayed his rustic ancestors, lying in Hambleton churchyard. The Demon had won. From the moment he stepped off the train at Woolwich a new life began.

Family Tree – It does not claim to be complete and is intended only to delineate most of the characters contained in the book

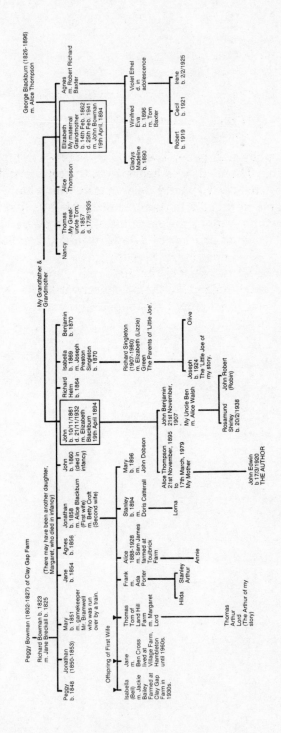